D0992413

American Wars, American Peace

American Wars,

PHILIP D. BEIDLER

Notes from a Son of the Empire

American Peace

The University of Georgia Press | Athens and London

© 2007 by the University of Georgia Press

Athens, Georgia 30602

All rights reserved

Set in Berthold Baskerville by Bookcomp, Inc.

Printed and bound by Maple-Vail

The paper in this book meets the guidelines for
permanence and durability of the Committee on
Production Guidelines for Book Longevity of the
Council on Library Resources.

Printed in the United States of America

11 10 09 08 07 C 5 4 3 2 1

Library of Congress Cataloging-in-Publication Data

Beidler, Philip D.

American wars, American peace : notes from a
son of the empire / Philip D. Beidler.

p. cm.

Includes bibliographical references.

ISBN-13: 978-0-8203-2969-7 (hardcover : alk. paper)

ISBN-10: 0-8203-2969-X (hardcover : alk. paper)

1. United States—Politics and government—1989–

2. United States—Politics and government—1945–1989.

3. United States—Military policy.

4. Imperialism.   5. War and society—United States.

6. Memory—Social aspects—United States.

7. Vietnam War, 1961–1975—Social aspects.

8. Iraq War, 2003– —Social aspects.

9. Beidler, Philip D.   10. Idealism, American.   I. Title.

E839.5.B413 2007

973.9—dc22   2007018939

British Library Cataloging-in-Publication Data available

In Memory of John F. Burnum, M.D.

ASN 14117989

Contents

Acknowledgments

I wish to thank the following people who helped me write this book: Donald Anderson, Joe Bageant, Celeste Burnum, Larry Goldstein, Belinda Gordon, Nancy Grayson, Mark Heberle, Richard Hyatt, Tim O'Brien, Andrea Porter, Steve Russell, Richard Summers, and the two outside readers selected by the University of Georgia Press. I also wish to express gratitude to the University of Alabama for ongoing support of my work, and to my wife, Ellen, and my daughter, Katherine, for constant encouragement and inspiration.

Acknowledgment is made for materials published in *Military History Magazine* and *Vietnam Magazine*.

American Wars, American Peace

Pax Americana

As in my previous book, *Late Thoughts on an Old War, American Wars, American Peace* comprises a set of linked essays combining personal memory and cultural reflection. The starting point in the earlier collection was the memory of my experience as an armored cavalry platoon leader in the Vietnam War. At the time, hovering over the text was the premonition of the Iraq War. It was a prophecy, a prediction, a catastrophe getting ready to happen. The essays in *American Wars, American Peace* often speak to the ways in which that vision has been realized.

Now, after nearly five years of major combat, the American war in Iraq presides, shadowlike, over the national consciousness as a new living nightmare, a kind of horrific eternal present. Everybody knows it's a mess, with its chief outcome the complication and exacerbation of long-standing cultural, religious, and geopolitical hatreds. Nobody much wants to think about it. Even the people who say they support it hate it. Aside from die-hard members of the party of memory—such as myself—who still want to ask about the complex apparatus of misperceptions and outright falsehoods brought forth to justify large-scale military commitment, not many people seem to remember how it began. Nobody wants to see one more telecast or read one more newspaper or internet story about a suicide bomber and three or four dead Americans and twenty or thirty dead Iraqis. Many cars on U.S. streets and highways still carry a fading emblem expressing support for our troops. Nearly no one, on the other hand, wants to send their husband or wife, brother or sister, son or daughter, nephew or niece, to get killed. There is barely enough interest left among Americans for mild rejoicing when the kingpin of insurgent violence is finally killed by an air force laser-guided bomb; outside Washington DC, nobody finds much occasion for cheering when the new democratic government in Baghdad momentarily gets Sunnis and Shia to agree on parceling out unfilled positions in a war cabinet.

Vietnam analogies abound. Many are appropriate. As part of post–September 2001 measures in the war against terror, an influential group of Washington DC militarists, at the highest levels of government, along with a president desirous of looking resolute and decisive on matters of national security, seeks authority from Congress to commit U.S. forces to battle against a foreign enemy. Dutifully, Congress—as in 1964, responding to a carefully orchestrated pretext of alleged attacks on U.S. naval vessels by North Vietnamese gunboats in the Gulf of Tonkin—approves a new war powers measure abrogating military authority to the White House and the Departments of Defense and State—this time on the basis of alleged Iraqi weapons of mass destruction and a purported Al Qaida connection. The result, to use an intentional mixed metaphor, is now a quagmire in the desert—as if anyone would know what the actual terrain of Iraq turns out to be: an alluvial basin in the south; gritty waste in the center, at present full of rubble-strewn cities; steppe and mountain in the north. The name of the mission is Pacification. Winning Hearts and Minds is now called Democracy Building. Vietnamization has been crystallized into a new Mesopotamian formula, packaged carefully in its articulation by politicians at home and commanders in the region: "As the Iraqis stand up we will stand down."

To be sure, for the people fighting it and for those among us directly connected to them, the new war breeds its peculiar horrors. The relatively larger casualty rolls of Vietnam, along with increasing problems with discipline, drugs, resistance to authority, and combat refusals, reflected the agonies of a conscript army. Here, our fighting force is described with substantial accuracy as professional and all-volunteer – albeit with enormous augmentation by reserve and national guard units. By now it is also, however, official protestations to the contrary, not unlike the old Vietnam army and marine units in the field, working on the edge of professional and psychological exhaustion. *Broken* is the word frequently used by military people – with army troops in Afghanistan and Iraq in their second and third combat tours and marines in their fourth and fifth. No politician dares mention the idea of a draft. Abroad, Islamic fundamentalists continue to mount savage, bloody terror attacks around the globe. At home, as nonstop information compels instant amnesia, global nightmare becomes devoid of history or memory.

The war is symptomatic. Americans squabble instead over a host of what are adeptly called hot-button issues – abortion, gay marriage, judicial appointments, religion in the schools – that become the focus of various forms of ideological obsession. Political, religious, educational, and cultural interest groups left and right resist any critical challenge to opinions and attitudes that might complicate their status as received truth. Weekly floods of commercials about movie releases contend with television autopsy and loincloth reality shows and the staged mayhem of the World Wrestling Federation. People watch the Super Bowl for the commercials. Must-have appurtenances and accessories come and go as quickly as the acronyms that describe them: DVDs, MP3s, iPods, PDAs, and SUVs. People get instantly rich enough on IPOs and hedge funds to build McMansions. Stocks, bonds, and various other traditional financial instruments yield to a new regime of expertise in the arcane mathematical economics of something called derivatives. Waves of corporate scandals result in courtroom trials of astonishingly wealthy defendants who spend tens of millions of dollars hiring battalions of lawyers and renting office spaces to house them. Apace, the salaries of executives continue to go stratospheric as the corporations they run fall into bankruptcy and their employee pension and health insurance funds go into meltdown. Las Vegas can't build new casinos and garish high-end resorts quickly enough. Mississippi and Louisiana have been trying to catch up since theirs were blown down by waves of hurricanes. Through the new real-estate stratagem of interest-only mortgages, people are encouraged to lay down enormous monthly payments for incredibly expensive houses on which they will accrue no cash value whatsoever. As consumer debt sky-rockets to somewhere between two and three trillion dollars, lenders— banks, finance corporations, credit-card companies—look for new ways to attract borrowers. Most months, borrowing increases by ten billion dollars. As the first members of the post–World War II baby boom generation reach their sixties, their sheer numbers and projected needs threaten to bankrupt the Social Security and Medicare systems, in the latter case not least beginning with the fact that forty percent of them are classified as clinically obese. (Meanwhile, the figure among the general population hovers at around thirty, with the overweight percentage around sixty.) In a world where the greatest part of humanity regularly goes hungry, U.S. food manufacturers, having worn out the latest diet fads, now invest in perfecting low-calorie products where the pleasure of fullness is achieved without nutrients being bodily metabolized. Drug prices go through the roof. A new, national government plan designed to help the indigent and the elderly with prescription expenses is so complicated that people have to be coerced into signing up. Once so coerced, millions of subscribers find themselves stranded without their daily medications when communications between the Medicare system and participating commercial health management organizations go hay-wire.

On the landscape of domestic culture, the nation becomes a world of bread and circuses undreamed. America's sport is NASCAR racing. Everything else from athletics to churchgoing turns out to be comparably rousing and spectacular. College football devotees learn to parse national championship ranking systems with the zeal of theologians and the discrimination of art critics, while even a marginal winning record ensures that any Division I team will participate in a bowl game somewhere. The latest Winter Olympic Games bring an upsurge in American medals, largely through the invention of bizarre, new, hotdog events and trends in athletic outfitting such as snowboarding and acrobatic skiing. TV viewers can download *American Idol* to their cell phones while watching Donald Trump humiliate people. Free therapy is available from Oprah or Doctor Phil. For those in search of higher forms of popular communion, megachurches routinely attract tens of thousands of worshippers to Sunday services, in one case held in a converted professional basketball arena where renovations costing $65 million included two waterfalls.

One is moved to retrospection. It wasn't supposed to turn out this way. Abroad, the new American legions garrison the far-flung outposts of the empire, with major fixed installations in roughly forty foreign nations extending from the current theaters of war in Iraq and Afghanistan to such old peacetime standbys as Korea, the United Kingdom, Germany, Belgium, Luxembourg, Spain, Italy, and Japan. Forward operational centers exist in Saudi Arabia, Kosovo, Bosnia, Colombia, Ecuador, El Salvador, Curaçao, and Aruba. Since 11 September 2001, U.S. troops have been deployed to assembly points in Kyrgyzstan, Uzbekistan, Tajikistan, Kuwait, Qatar, Turkey, and Bulgaria. A major new naval installation occupies the island of Diego Garcia in the Indian Ocean. Manning seven hundred major bases abroad and six thousand more in the United States and its overseas territories, in the fifth year of the first Afghan War and the fourth year of the second Iraq war, we stand at the frontiers. And we need to. Around the globe, since 11 September 2001, we have been at real war against real enemies who wish our destruction. Whatever phase of our history began on that day, and whatever courses of response we have taken, whether appropriate, as it now seems, in the offensive against Al Qaida and the Taliban in Afghanistan, or ill-advised, as in the overthrow of the Saddam Hussein regime in Iraq, it began on that date with military enemies who availed themselves of the possibilities of the most free and open society in history to attack us; and our legitimate response was to hunt them down wherever they were in the world and kill them. How can one say it otherwise? We are the new Romans; and this is Pax Americana.

Still, the reader is entitled to an explanation for the phrasing. What kind of person, amid the political and military circumstances detailed above, devises a phrasing like Pax Americana? The short answer would be an ironist. Or, in a slightly more academic turn, perhaps a literary antiquarian who has read enough Tacitus on the Roman conquests to know that the famous words about making a desert and calling it peace are not those of the author but his Latin transliteration of those of the chieftain of a conquered people – as it happens, an ancient Briton, describing the Romans and speaking in a language now lost to history and memory. Or, in the broadest sense, maybe just a person who has experienced and remembered enough of history to reflect on the kinds of peace that one empire after another has tried to impose on the world at whatever immense costs of fear, suffering, destruction, and death.

Such explanations are all true in their way. At the same time, I hope the subtitle of this book makes it clear that any answer to the question – for an American such as myself writing as a beneficiary of post–World War II American peace and prosperity – is meant to carry particular generational meanings as well. "A true son of the empire": this is what the narrator-protagonist Philip Dosier calls himself in Larry Heinemann's novel of Vietnam combat, *Close Quarters*. For those of us who served there, and who have now lived out the ensuing cycles of American wars and American peace, surely the phrase gets more personal and more representative and more telling with each passing year. "I grew out of one war and into another," writes Tim O'Brien in his Vietnam War memoir, *If I Die in a Combat Zone*. "My father came from leaden ships of sea, from the Pacific Theater; my mother was a WAVE. I was the offspring of the great campaign against the tyrants of the 1940s." For a chapter in which he describes standing night guard over three old Vietnamese men, staked upright as interrogation suspects, he presciently selects the title "Centurion." Other chapter titles include "Pro Patria," "Mori," and "Dulce et Decorum." Ron Kovic, echoing composer George M. Cohan, titled his bitter account of the war *Born on the Fourth of July*. "Ask not what your country can do for you—ask what you can do for your country," he quotes John Kennedy as saying on a first epigraph page, pairing it with his own dismal echo of a lyric:

I am the living death
the memorial day on wheels
I am your yankee doodle dandy
your john wayne come home
your fourth of july firecracker
exploding in the grave.

Updating the musical reference to Creedence Clearwater Revival, the late Lewis Puller, son of the most decorated marine in corps history, called his autobiography *Fortunate Son.* Now this title is beyond sadness: Puller, a multiple amputee from combat wounds, relapsed into alcoholism after the publication of the book and eventually took his own life with a gunshot to the head.

But beyond my cohort of the war, I also mean to invoke the memory of all the sons and daughters of the republic who once saw themselves in a larger sense as the new American generation of youth: the baby-boom progeny of the "Greatest Generation" who at home and abroad became the foot soldiers (a term they would have readily embraced) of the Peace Corps, the civil rights movement, the antiwar movement, the antinuclear movement, the women's movement, the gay rights movement, the environmental movement. I mean all of us who once believed in the promise of America in everyday people's lives, of making us citizens of what Jefferson called the Empire of Liberty.

For many of us, the depth of all this could be revealed in the myriad stories we had of coming of age in midcentury America, stories that formed a larger, inherited vision of national purpose. My own memories dated from growing up as a son of a Quaker and a Mennonite within sight of the Gettysburg battlefield. In the 1950s you could still hear the plant whistles and sirens go off in small towns at the eleventh hour of the eleventh day of the eleventh month of the year. Armistice Day, we called it then. And after that came V-E and V-J Day, and in childhood many of us were surrounded by community leaders, high school teachers, coaches, bandleaders, family members, and family friends who had been with the marines in the Pacific or the army in Europe. One of my uncles had been a B-17 pilot; another had been an army field medic in Italy; a teacher had been a marine in the Pacific; a neighbor had flown the Ploiesti raid in Romania; a family friend had been a navy submariner. I genuinely believe that, as legatees of such people, many members of my generation have now spent their lives trying to honor those gifts of duty and sacrifice by keeping ourselves awake to the challenge they also bequeathed us: that of trying to understand and exercise with justice to all people the terms and conditions of our nation's unprecedented power and responsibilities in the world. We grew up believing that to be a post–World War II American was to hold on to some necessary idea of the meanings and obligations of being a person in history.

In just this relation to some new idea of noble post-1945 American mission, it remains part of our collective, cultural memory that the Empire State Building was the tallest structure in the world while my generation was growing up. Its height was later topped, and now the twin towers have come down. At the beginning of the millennium, this is in every respect astonishing. Who would have dreamed that, out of a ruinous and catastrophic century of ideological world war and human annihilation, with nuclear holocaust in several instances barely avoided, the globe would now plunge itself into a new, even more unspeakable dark age of terror? In all these respects, such things are now felt with a peculiar sense of failure and elegiac poignancy, I believe, by those of us of the post–World War II American generation who believed we might make good on the promises of our elders to the world. We are beginning to get old now. A lot of us died or lost great pieces of ourselves along the way. It is not at all as we believed it would turn out to be.

But for a writer, there is also more. To put it directly, one simply cannot doubt that, in a new age of electronic, instant-information amnesia, one writes increasingly in the awareness of chronicling one's own historical obsolescence. Still, a writer writes. A writer does this, I believe, for the reason adduced by Rick Bragg in telling his family story about a violent, impoverished childhood in northeastern Alabama, all the while knowing that when he got done it wouldn't matter one way or the other—a reason he says he learned as a police reporter in New Orleans from a black woman in the projects whose child had been killed one morning by a stray bullet as he stood in the doorway waiting to go to school. Bragg watched, he records, as she pulled out a wrinkled scrapbook of newspaper clippings about the incident. "People remembers it," she says. "People forgets if it ain't wrote down." "I reckon," Bragg remembers saying. That was enough for him. It is still enough for me—even if it probably isn't true.

Top Gun and the Tank Driver

Consider this essay a species of history. Actually, I insist—even as the dying from the catastrophic U.S. war in Iraq has gone on for so long that what I attempt to record here will never amount to anything more than a bizarre, reflexive anecdote.

Still, I make my claim. I insist that we commit to national memory the fact that the following things happened, in a kind of dreadful synchronicity on 1 May 2003, the forty-third day of the second Iraq War: On one side of the globe, George W. Bush, the president of the United States, was engaging in a publicity stunt triumphantly depositing him from the copilot seat of a navy jet to the deck of an aircraft carrier in the

Pacific Ocean off San Diego, California. More or less simultaneously, on the other side of the same world, a U.S. Army enlisted man was drowning near Baghdad, Iraq, when a riverbank gave way under the weight of the M-1 tank he was driving, tipping the tank into the river and trapping him underwater. Later the parallel narratives would reunite in a second appalling convergence. In a Memorial Day speech more than a year after what became known as the Top Gun stunt, the president quoted, for patriotic inspiration, letters from the dead tank driver.

Here was the whole monstrous idiocy of the Iraq scheme in microcosm, a real-life allegory of the absurd. Yet, even as I wrote, I knew that I was racing against history *and* memory. The public or political part of the story involving George W. Bush—the carrier stunt, the groundless declaration of victory six weeks into a war that would still be going on nearly three years later—was old stuff, at the time much exploited for its news potential and then thoroughly worked over in subsequent cultural discussion. So, pretty much from the beginning, was the private or personal part involving the tank driver, which might for a brief period have had a certain human interest, as they used to say, but probably was not of sufficient historical or even journalistic currency to carry anything more than its own weight. That story, too, was a dead letter.

Meanwhile, I knew I was also writing a set of notes toward my own obsolescence. Over a career of thirty years I had talked about the impossibility of writing history in a country where everything more or less has always been history—as in, "oh yes, but that's history." More recently, I had begun to question the possibility even of how we can discuss memory, let alone history, in a country where no fact or story lives much longer than a text message, a cell phone call, or a CNN headline. History was gone. Memory was gone. For all that, I was still writing about the real deal. The real deal remains our need to know what it means to be a person in a world where thoughts and actions have consequences for other humans. I would write something called "Top Gun and the Tank Driver" because I thought somebody needed to tie together these two stories as part of the record of this terrible war.

Of all military events taking place on that day in 2003, the most visible was surely the jet landing being made by George W. Bush, the

American commander in chief, on a U.S. Navy aircraft carrier, where, after bopping around on the deck in a borrowed G-suit and exchanging high fives with the flight crew, he gave a speech in which he announced "the end of major combat operations" in the theater of war. The carrier, the USS *Abraham Lincoln*, was returning from the war zone nearly half a world away, where its aircraft, as part of a lightning defeat of Iraqi military forces, had been responsible for dropping an estimated one-third of the aerial ordnance used on the enemy. Right down to a banner above the deck reading "MISSION ACCOMPLISHED," the cocky flyboy message was lost on no one.

The occasion was a giddy takeoff on the final victory scene from the 1986 Tom Cruise–Val Kilmer movie *Top Gun*. The heroic loner–the brave but dangerous Maverick (Cruise)–has just shot down two Russian MIG-29s. Two navy F-14 Tomcat fighters come roaring in for landings on an aircraft carrier flight deck and, amid the cheering of deck crews, Maverick is reunited with the equally brave but by-the-book Iceman (Kilmer). "You can be my wingman any day," the latter bellows in the midst of a long-delayed buddy embrace. Arriving by chopper on the deck are the crewmen of an F-14 shot down by a MIG. They are miraculously unwounded. The pesky MIGs and their pilots, of course, are toast. Still damp from their dunking but otherwise unscathed, however, their good-guy American victims hop out of the rescue chopper and join the deckwide celebration.

In the 2003 version, the president's costuming, swagger, and air of easy familiarity proclaimed that he, like Maverick and Iceman, had been around a jet plane or two in his life and felt comfortable in the company of elite aviators and aircrew. And indeed, his military service record included Vietnam War–era pilot training and sporadic fighter duty with the Texas Air National Guard–in the American South. On the *Abraham Lincoln*, the president was thus putting a "MISSION ACCOM-PLISHED" period to doubt on a number of things beyond immediate war aims: his own military credentials; his image as a war president; his judgment in extending a post–September 2001 American war on terror-ism into an internationally dubious preemptive invasion of a sovereign Arab nation; even, one might have surmised, to a note of unfinished business left by his father in allowing the Saddam Hussein regime to remain after the equally quick and decisive victory of U.S. forces in Operation Desert Storm nearly fifteen years earlier.

The second military newsmaker of 1 May 2003 was a U.S. Army private first class, killed in Iraq when his M-1 Abrams tank rolled down a collapsing riverbank of the Euphrates River near Habbinayah, overturning in the water and trapping and drowning him. As with all preliminary casualty reports, his name and other personal information were withheld pending family notification. They were disclosed later that month. He was Jesse Givens, age thirty-four, of Springfield, Missouri. A tank driver, he was a member of the Second Squadron, Third Armored Cavalry Regiment, based at Fort Carson, Colorado, from which he and his unit had deployed on 11 April. Among the oldest in the army, the regiment had shot its way into Iraq, a journey that had figured heavily in live television and newspaper reports because of the reporters embedded with the unit. Givens, somewhat old for a PFC, had been predictably nicknamed Grandpa and Pops by his buddies but had been regarded as capable and enthusiastic. The former high school wrestler and football player, smiling and shaven-headed in his photographs, with the kind of big build that used to be called burly, was decidedly up to the physical and mental challenge. According to some accounts, Givens had decided to make his career in the army and was in the pipeline for officer training. Subsequent obituary reflections differed on whether he had been laid off as a metalworker or, motivated by patriotism, had quit his job and enlisted. His wife, Melissa, the mother of Givens's five-year-old stepson, Dakota, was pregnant with their child, due in June (son Carson, presumably named for the fort, was born 29 May). Living near base, she got the news of Givens's death from an official, uniformed army visitation team, as specified in the procedures concerning family notification and condolence. The visit came roughly an hour after Bush made his official announcement about the end of hostilities.

The Top Gun story was big news—not just that day but the next and the next and several days after that. The analysts analyzed and the commentators commented. Sure, most concluded that it was a shameless publicity stunt, but its partisan political motives and election-year implications had to be weighed against its positive value as a boost to the morale of the troops and of the American public. A few lonely voices were heard among Democrats. On the senate floor, Robert Byrd of West Virginia held forth: "To me it is an affront to the Americans killed and injured in Iraq for the president to exploit the trappings of war for the momentary spectacle of a speech." In the house, Representative Henry Waxman of California called for a Government Accounting Office inquiry into the cost of the event to taxpayers. Byrd's and Waxman's comments were written off as partisan politics from veteran complainers, both Democrats, who had been vociferously antiwar and antiadministration from the beginning.

Debate fell to particular mission details. What was the commander-in-chief president doing flying from Washington DC to California to land on an aircraft carrier steaming the other way in the Pacific Ocean? Why did he risk a tailhook landing–albeit in the copilot seat of an S-3B Viking, a slow, stable VIP jet–when a standard presidential helicopter delivery would have been safer and less complicated in terms of where the ship was going and why? (Everyone breathed a sigh of relief when the Viking landed safely, including then–National Security Advisor Condoleeza Rice, photographed in her own goofy little deck helmet.) For that matter, what was the carrier doing out there waiting for the president in the first place? White House spokespeople started falling all over themselves. Their first explanation was that the carrier was too far offshore for a helicopter. It was returning, moreover, from a nearly ten-month deployment, and the president certainly didn't want to "inconvenience" the crew. In fact, the news quickly emerged that the carrier had been not only just thirty miles offshore–completely within helicopter range–but had been slowed down and kept circling there, essentially on hold, for the plane landing. Well, the carrier had arrived at the rendezvous point sooner, White House Spokesman Ari Fleisher explained, than weather reports would have suggested. Why still the jet instead of the helicopter? Fleisher got right back to Reuters: "The president wanted to land on it, on an aircraft that would allow him to see an aircraft landing the same way that the pilots see an aircraft landing. He wanted to see it as realistically as possible." Fleisher didn't explain how the president's desire to see an aircraft landing from the pilot's perspective accounted for the previous day's practice in emergency underwater survival skills in the White House swimming pool; or for the care taken with the temporary stenciling on the plane's cockpit liner—just like Maverick's or Iceman's—of the name and rank of its VIP passenger; or for the precise angling of the carrier during the landing itself, so as not to reveal in photos the profile of San Diego's high buildings in the background. These and other questions apparently remained unasked, and certainly unanswered. Like, how come nobody ever wants to see what an infantryman sees as realistically as possible? The president's fancy would have hardly required an aircraft carrier, still making slow circles in a fifteen-hour trip that could have been covered in one.

The Tank Driver story, of military necessity, began to come out gradually only in later days and weeks. And even then it was "big news" only in the news markets relative to PFC Givens's life. By the end of that first week in May 2003, death notices appeared in local papers in Missouri, where he had grown up, and Colorado, his last stateside duty station where he had lived with his wife. In Missouri his brother described him as "a great man, kind of the hero type, always helping the underdog. He didn't care for people picking on people. He had a good heart." Colorado reports centered on the dead soldier's happy relationships with Melissa, her son Dakota, and even their already personified unborn child. A 10 May follow-up story on local television covered the funeral ceremony held at Fort Carson, where Melissa received posthumous awards on behalf of her husband: the Bronze Star with a "V" device for Valor and the Army Commendation Medal for Meritorious Service. A similar notice eventually appeared in the Springfield, Missouri, *New Tribune* about a memorial service to be held there 30 June.

Back in Colorado, the story continued, parallel with others, in a *Rocky Mountain Times* article of 2 August 2003 including an account, along with those of other bereaved Fort Carson widows, of Melissa Givens's experience with the official casualty notification process. But then something big happened. On Veterans Day, 11 November, the *New York Times* printed letters from three dead American soldiers that centered on premonitions of death in Iraq and the possible meanings of such sacrifice. One was a letter from Jesse Givens to his wife, Melissa. It expressed a "true" and "natural" father's love for his stepson Dakota. It addressed the unborn child they had jokingly decided to name Bean, because that's what he had looked like on the last ultrasound they saw together. And it concluded with thanks to Melissa for a marriage that, he professed, had been a marriage "for a million lifetimes." "Please find it in your heart to forgive me for leaving you alone," he said. "Take care of yourself, believe in yourself, you are a strong, big hearted woman. Teach our babies to love life to its fullest tell yourself to do the same. Don't forget to take Toad [Dakota] to Disney World. I will be there with you. Melissa I will always want you need you and love you in my heart, mind, and soul. Do me a favor, after you tuck Toad and Bean in, give them hugs and kisses from me. Go outside and look at the stars and count them. Don't forget to smile."

Meanwhile, Givens's name and personal information were posted on a Web site titled "Fallen Heroes of Iraqi Freedom." Expressions of sympathy poured in from around the country. As with the news stories, the tone of response combined patriotic sentiment with quiet respect for personal sacrifice. Web postings accumulated, running to around twenty print pages. They came from sympathetic strangers, members of fellow military families, people who read Givens's letter in the *New York Times*, or, in one case, a person who heard Givens's *New York Times* letter read aloud in church. They included song lyrics (including an opening entry, provided in a note by Givens's mother, from Jesse's favorite band, Diamond Rio), inspirational poetry, and scripture. Melissa Givens responded on the Web with expressions of gratitude, both to anonymous correspondents and to family members – her own mother and father, as well as various in-laws – who appeared as regular contributors. She also began writing and posting letters to her dead husband.

Back in the print media, a Christmas feature from Denver television on 22 December 2003 featured Melissa reading from the text printed in the *New York Times* and from other letters Givens had written prior to his death. Several months later, on 19 March 2004, came an extensive follow-up, focusing on the widowed young mother, now with their two sons, and revealing the background stories on a number of Givens's letters. Three, in particular, got detailed coverage; one, recently written but unsent, had been found on Givens's body; one had been more carefully preserved—the "in case of my death" missive reprinted in the national media—in his wallet; and another, written and posted, had arrived after his death. Also cited were journal entries Melissa had found, written at home before Givens's deployment, revealing his attitudes and values, his awareness of the possibility he might die, and his appreciation for all that he was leaving behind. Here, Givens himself now continued to speak from beyond the grave—actually proving, the headlines contended, that the pen could be mightier than the sword. Irony was nowhere in the picture. On Saturday, 1 May 2004, these materials became the basis of a feature story on National Public Radio's *Weekend Edition.* Included was an audio reproduction from the television video of Melissa reading from Givens's letters.

One last appearance in the media spotlight, however, was still to come. And when it happened, it was national in a big way. On Memorial Day, 31 May 2004, the commander in chief gave a speech in Arlington National Cemetery at the Tomb of the Unknowns. He closed his speech by quoting a number of letters from fallen veterans. The last cited came from PFC Jesse Givens. It was the famous wallet letter. To his stepson, Dakota, the president quoted Givens as saying "I will always be there in our park when you dream, so we can play." To his wife, Melissa, he repeated his instruction that she count the stars and remember to smile. "This is the quality of our people in uniform," the president concluded, movingly, to warm applause.

It was the final turn in an utterly bizarre scenario that could not have been dreamed up by a postmodern metafictionist. In rhetorical obliviousness of its perfect synchronicity with the 1 May 2003 big story of President George W. Bush's USS *Abraham Lincoln* fly-in and victory celebration, the White House spin machine had brought the 1 May 2003 nonstory about the death of PFC Jesse Givens full circle, thoroughly homogenized, and raked over for its made-for-media potential in yet another media event.

The mishap in Iraq that killed PFC Jesse Givens was a strange one, especially for an Abrams tank driver who had survived a month of sustained offensive combat against opposing Iraqi forces. It was what is generally called an accident of war – even among soldiers something definitely back page and fairly routine – in this case part of a war that was starting to get old. As in a death by drowning, the victim was unmarked by the usual gross stigmata of war – bullet or fragmentation wounds, evidence of burning, instant disintegration, traumatic limb separations, broken bones, head injuries, crushed entrails. Anyone who has been in a war knows firsthand that there are too many ironic ways to die, none of which in and of themselves make much of a story – a point that Erich Maria Remarque enforced definitively in 1929 by titling his World War I novel *All Quiet on the Western Front.* Actually, the German title – *Im Westen Nichts Neu* – translates better: "in the west, nothing new." It is the formula for a standard radio report on days with little combat action.

Invest the Givens fatality with what ironies one might, still, it called attention to itself as a particularly vital statistic in a larger context of numbers that, once put in the spotlight, should probably not be allowed to disappear. That number is the casualty count of dead American soldiers on 1 May 2003, which the president had declared the day of victory. It is, officially, 128 killed. PFC Givens was the 129th. On 30 January 2005, widely heralded democratic elections were held in Iraq. American combat formations were still deployed in roughly the numbers present in the original invading force. The death toll of those killed in action stood at around fifteen hundred. On the day of the elections, much was made of an approximately sixty percent voter turnout. Less noted was that fifty Iraqi civilians died the same day in terrorist-related violence. No one really knows the current Iraqi death toll from the war except to say that as of this writing it continues to rise by fifty or a hundred more on any given day. Meanwhile, the wounded are, as journalists say, another story. It is estimated that, out of around ten thousand U.S. combat casualties, half will continue to require treatment for the indeterminate future. No one has the foggiest notion of Iraqis injured by combat or terrorist violence. A standard statistical procedure used by the military is to take the death factor and enlarge it by three or five to one.

On 31 May 2004 the commander in chief had given his "count the stars" Memorial Day Speech at the Tomb of the Unknowns in Arlington.

Another part of the day's patriotic celebration—with another big media tie-in—was the dedication of a big, elaborate, official monument on the National Mall in Washington honoring the U.S. veterans of World War II, fifty-nine years after that war ended. Planners arranged events so as to try to link the present with the re-creation of an earlier kind of Memorial Day when the grandchildren of World War II veterans were not fighting and dying in Iraq, but rather when the World War II vets themselves, like veterans before them, were young men and women just back from duty. The speakers that day said that each of us, in such times as these, whether in uniform or not, needed to be more like the greatest generation—just as they had once been like the great generation or generations before them.

That was once how I felt about Memorial Day, too. In a small-town cemetery in Adams County, Pennsylvania, on a hillside from which one could see all the way into Gettysburg, and then to Culp's Hill and the Round Tops on the battlefield beyond, on Memorial Day we annually looked history-ward and beyond. I can still see the shell-shocked World War I veteran who always led the parade up to the cemetery, and the flatbed truck draped with bunting from which the mayor made a short speech, and kids from the grade school recited Lincoln's Gettysburg Address and John MacCrae's "In Flanders Fields." I was one of those children. Most vividly, I see the VFW honor guard of World War II vets, my father's friends, maybe straining the bellies of their old Eisenhower jackets but for the most part still young, vigorous, happy men with hopeful lives before them. Memorial Days were the stuff of heroes. Then came my war, Vietnam.

Now I hate every Memorial Day, no matter which president presides over it. Now I hate patriotic holidays that compel people to recite the connections between today's honored dead and those of the last war, and the one before that, and the one before that. Maybe, in the midst of the current war, with the casualty rosters waiting to be read in the newspaper every day, I just feel guilty all over again, like anyone who has made it through combat, that I'm alive and a lot of other people are not. Or maybe I'm fed up with hearing speeches from people who don't know any better, profaning the memory of people who almost always, at least as I remember it in the decades since I came home, died scared and alone holding their wounds, or with piss and shit running down their legs, or with chunks of them blown off—or even drowned in an overturned tank.

The president and his people who staged the 2003–4 shows aboard the *Abraham Lincoln* and later at Arlington National Cemetery eventually managed to earn themselves a new set of Memorial Days. Whatever they have kept coming up with, all I can say is that any such ritual over which this president presides as commander in chief will always remind me mainly of one thing: Top Gun. Not *Top Gun*, the movie. But Top Gun, the goddamn aircraft carrier stunt when a president of the United States and his political image-makers decided to declare victory in the latest American war. I still see that banner above the deck: "MISSION ACCOMPLISHED." Sure, they wish *now* they hadn't done it, as even Carl Rove finally admitted. I'll bet they'd like to scoop up every video of it in existence. But I think it ought to be shown every day until this terrible war is over—like the Abu Ghraib prison photos, shown over and over and over, with the naked, squirming captives, and all the overgrown American boys and girls from the hollows and hamlets of southern Pennsylvania, the Maryland panhandle, and West Virginia; then all the shots of hollow-eyed army grunts and marines, in their sand-colored fatigues, stalking through the sand-colored rubble toward the next sniper or ambush; then the dress portraits of all the dead ones, in their army greens or marine blues, looking so young and sheepishly cocky; then all the Iraqis—the guy from the ambushed van of recruits with the matted entrance wound in the temple, or the dead father of nine who got a head full of shrapnel while, after bringing poll workers tea and cakes, he waited to vote. Set up right beside them ought to be the video of our helmeted, flight-suited commander in chief, lately of the Texas Air National Guard. Not that it will probably matter to anyone other than me at this point, now months and years removed.

Memorial Day: for me I think it will always be just the most recent remake of a bad war movie. Fully a decade ago I tried to illuminate such a difference between wars and war movies in an essay I called "Just Like in the Movies: Richard Nixon and *Patton*," which was based on my personal experiences as a platoon leader in the Vietnam War. It concerned a day late in my tour in Vietnam when my unit lost a lot of people killed and wounded in an ambush, with the dead including our much-admired brigade commander, a one-star GI general killed about a hundred and fifty feet from me down a no-name dusty road. *His* letters to his wife were also posthumously published in U.S. newspapers, which I discovered only later because at the time of their publication I myself was not yet, as we used to phrase it, "back in world." The essay juxtaposed my memories of that day with my discovery, decades later while doing research on old World War II movies, that on the same day as our high-casualty ambush in Vietnam, back in Washington DC our Commander in Chief Richard Nixon was nerving himself for the Cambodian invasion by getting drunk with his buddies and repeatedly viewing George C. Scott's cinematic performance in *Patton*. The essay concluded with observations about the difference between war movies and war as it is experienced on the battlefield that seemed so bizarre and obvious that I felt silly making the point. It was the last thing I hoped I would ever have to write on why American presidents, of all people, who make terrible, life-and-death decisions about war and peace on a geopolitical scale, should not confuse what they see in movies with what happens in wars. Now, at the risk of seeming bizarre and obvious again, I find I have to repeat it. "If it is reprehensible for people to die in war," I wrote then, "it is even more reprehensible for them to die because of someone's failure to distinguish between a war and a war movie. That is an elementary observation, as obvious and painful now as it should have been twenty-five years ago." Make that thirty-five, and counting.

On the edge of the end of the print revolution, as we move into the world of instant, nonstop, inundating cyberdata, it is the way of information now more than ever that things sort themselves out within months and days—even hours and minutes—into the relatively significant and insignificant. And the way of information is usually by the numbers: one tank driver; as of late 2006, around three thousand U.S. combat fatalities; at least 25,000, and perhaps as many as 100,000 Iraqi dead—including, as briefly reported, fifty who died on 30 January 2005. Earlier that same month, 200,000 tsunami victims; during the period of active American military engagement in Indochina, 58,000 U.S. troops and two to four million Vietnamese; during the Third Reich, six million Jews.

The blur of data notwithstanding, particular things need to be remembered about every particular war. These things need to be remembered about this terrible war: There were no weapons of mass destruction found in Iraq. There was no direct terrorist connection between the dictatorship of Saddam Hussein and Al Qaida. We invaded another sovereign nation because our government decided it needed a change of government over there. That was the way the war came to be. For the American soldiers committed to battle by their commander in chief, the war has not played out like a Tom Cruise–Val Kilmer movie. Those who have died so far did so one by one by one, often in painful and inglorious ways. That is how it happened. And that is the way it needs to be written.

Sons and Fathers, Bad Wars and Good Wars

My friend John, the wise and learned physician, never lived a day without knowing how completely he had been part of the generation of 1945. When asked throughout his life for a biographical sketch of some sort, he invariably began by describing himself as a career practitioner of internal medicine and a survivor of the Battle of the Bulge. That was the way he phrased it: a doctor of medicine and a survivor of the Battle of the Bulge. At the same time, he made light of his military credentials to the degree that the only decoration posted on his office wall—purposely put there so people might ask about it—was a medal he had won for high school bandsmanship. That was John in abstract or epitome:

accomplished, honored, even illustrious in his profession, a survivor of the Battle of the Bulge who had once excelled at ninth-grade clarinet.

By any standard, when arrhythmia took John in his sleep in the summer of 2005, he had been a shining example of the generation who had come back to make something better of their world from the terrible war that had sent them to North Africa, Italy, and Western Europe, to Alaska, East Asia, and the Pacific. At this, he had been successful. His had been what people used to call a good life. A local youth and graduate of the hometown state university with a Harvard M.D., he had spent decades, practicing into his late seventies, as the dean of the local medical community, an internist with a respected practice, a teaching physician on the medical school faculty, an author in major professional journals, and a charming and funny occasional writer—the kind of medical eminence who might as easily have been at home at the Mayo Clinic, Massachusetts General, or some other world-class academic center. He found marital and familial happiness; as much material success and security as mattered; a rich cultural life as a reader, writer, concert- and lecture-goer, patron of the arts; the reputation as an active contributor to community projects. He occasionally liked cutting and trimming in his wife's English garden. An inveterate trash picker upper, he responded to some old GI basic-training impulse in him by doing weekly police calls in the neighborhood, sharing proudly the results of what he called anecdotal market research, identifying by relative numbers of empties the latest student preferences in canned beer. He looked like a big, loping, loose-shirted, long-footed boy whether in his yard clothes, with a big sun hat for all the skin cancers his dermatologist kept carving off, or, as frequently, in his tennis whites, chugging out to play Wednesday and weekend afternoons with his crafty old doubles friends.

In all these respects, it was easy to visualize John seventy or more years earlier, gangly and intent, as the youthful protagonist of an anecdote he enjoyed telling, one about carrying a bunch of curious rocks across town to the university geology department one summer day, where he found a scholarly looking older man in one of the labs who put down his work and took several hours to help him sort and identify what turned out to be the most common sorts of mud and minerals. It launched his love for the university, he said. His quondam lab instructor had been the venerable and distinguished state geologist himself. In old age, John himself was notably playful, whimsical with children, conducting conversations over the years with my daughter on the finer points of imaginary woodland and garden creatures.

With the long, starched white coat on, the pressed button-down shirt, the immaculately tied bow tie, he looked positively imperial. Trusted, revered, even beloved by many patients, he was no doubt remembered by some for a dispassionate, perhaps forbidding, reserve. Especially in late life, the whole identity came together in the image of a senator or philosopher of classical antiquity. Tall, angular, gracefully slim, with chiseled patrician features, a fringe of graying hair above a noble brow, John represented something lofty and fine, in the best sense of the word, magisterial.

In the public world, with his wife, he was an archetype of the citizen for whom the phrase *town and gown* was probably crafted. He had been an undergraduate engineering major. Well along in his medical career he had become a writer of major policy documents for a university president who had gone to Washington DC as the secretary of the Department of Health, Education, and Welfare. In the dimension of academic life at the university, he and his wife had established an endowed award for faculty excellence in scholarship, regarded as the university's premier research and writing prize. Such prizes are not uncommon, but this one carried the stipulation that no candidate was to be considered who was not also an accomplished teacher.

I had been fortunate enough to win that award well into my own third decade at the university. I saw it then and now as the crown of my career. But the award paled beside our friendship. John and I lived next door to each other in the old part of town, on a thickly wooded domain still preserved amid houses and businesses. It was there that his fanciful taxonomic conversations with my daughter took place. He and I talked a lot as well. I was an academic, grateful and loyal to the university for the opportunities it had allowed me. I was a former combat soldier, an armored cavalryman from the Vietnam War. I was a writer, and we would talk often about that. John would sometimes call me up with a piquant grammar or usage problem. What's the deal with this "different than" business, as opposed to "different from"? Is there an official position on "hopefully"? Since when did people start dropping the *ue* ending off a word like *catalogue*? When you use the word *whomever* in a relative clause, how do you make sure the reader understands that you know what you're doing? I often read his work in draft before he sent it to journals. He always wanted to see any kind of general-interest thing I was working on.

That John had made a good life was something of a wonder, because he had had a very bad war. About to be drafted near the end of college, he volunteered for an ASTP (Advanced Special Training Program), meaning that he was a candidate for officer training or a technical assignment. But in December 1944 the Germans attacked one last time in the west, launching a terrifying offensive against weak U.S. formations in Belgium and Luxembourg. His entire training platoon was sent to a replacement depot in France. Trucked from there to the front lines, the next day he found himself with a rifle in an icy hole in the Ardennes, along a line thinly held by the remnants of the Ninety-ninth Division. It was freezing. There was nobody else around. The German artillery was nonstop. The Americans were not firing back. On nights long after the war, his wife told me, he could still hear German tanks squeaking their way across the snow. Sometimes he woke up, she said, and moved from window to window. "They're out there," he would tell her. "They're out there."

Some of his closest friends remained those of his hometown youth, especially if they had been through a version of combat such as he remembered. One in particular was descended from an old southern German merchant family. Stan was a Jew who had walked across France and into Germany as an enlisted rifleman, living in daily fear of being captured. He too had become an important man, a well-known and influential businessperson and civic leader. But when the two of them were together, they got along, quietly, simply, affectionately. The doctor didn't like blowhards or people who threw their weight around. As a former enlisted man, martinets were out as well.

He seemed so thoroughly to have redeemed his war. Only toward the end, to use Tim O'Brien's phrasing about my war ("the things they carried"), did I begin to learn some of the other things he had borne within for the rest of his life. One was a story of twentieth-century American manhood, filtered through the alembic of what might be called the history of the South, yet strangely all the more American for that. Another was the story of a man who literally spent his life finding out who he was. Save for a name and some family history, John never knew his father. He just knew that his mother had divorced early and remarried. Of his biological father, John knew that he had been a son of farming people and had followed family tradition by going to the state agricultural and military college. Photographs of the father in uniform as a cadet and officer took full measure of what seemed to be a natural military bearing, that lofty erectness, that look in the eye of cold command. He too had left university to go to war, finishing his studies afterward. John's father had planned to be a career officer, and he had gotten off to a start as a bona fide hero of the American Expeditionary Force in the trenches of France during World War I. In the military they had a saying about someone who had "had a good war," being in the right battle at the right time, getting coveted decorations, catching an important person's eye. In those respects, the father had had a good war. Unfortunately, he had been badly wounded and gassed, with the latter ruining his lungs so as to render him unfit for further service. Upon his return home he married a belle, a famed beauty. He drifted about postwar life for ten years, drinking heavily, fighting lung disease, and struggling with bouts of madness. In his thirties he went upstairs and put on his uniform, then used his military service revolver to shoot himself in the head.

John remembered, from around age twelve, one strange, solitary, mournful trip by train to meet his father's people. Otherwise, in the course of his life, he had simply tried to work through that part of him, to understand and accept it as part of a great mysterious sadness that lay somewhere far in his past, and left it at that. But then, a few years back, something new and important had come to him from that past: relatives, cleaning out family relics, had sent him a huge trove of his father's effects from World War I. There was a complete set of combat gear: a doughboy helmet, a gas mask, trench goggles, an officer's Sam

Browne belt, and an over-the-top brass whistle. There was also a cache of letters from the young officer to his mother.

John delved into all this, sorted it out, and undertook to reshape it into a kind of tribute—if not to the honor and glory of his dead father, at least to a sense of memory and connection. He had the memorabilia and elegantly legible samples of the letters carefully photographed. He arranged these with photos of his father in uniform, formal portraits as cadet and officer, group shots with comrades in France, a few from after the war, with his father in civilian clothes, one from a newspaper where his father had come out to a local airfield to meet an old friend from the trenches, a pioneering aviator who would go on to command World War II U.S. bomber forces in England. All this he bookended with family portraits, then and now: of his parents and grandparents; of himself and his wife with their children and grandchildren. He organized everything, together with a narrative of his own composition, into a handsome, nicely typeset, crafted, and illustrated book, produced by a local printer. The narrative was mainly a biography of his father; but it also included reflections on his motives in assembling such a text.

He noted that his father had been a loyal and courageous officer who cared about his men. He observed with amusement that in letters home his father had been candid but not too graphic about what he was going through, often with attempts to make dire matters humorous. John wondered about what it might have been like for them to talk, soldier to soldier. "I wish," he concluded, "that we had known each other. Things might have turned out differently."

After forty-five years, he had given up his medical practice only to plunge into a postretirement career as a teaching physician, making rounds every morning with third- and fourth-year medical students and interns, and supervising and mentoring residents. Then, two months before his death, he learned that he had to quit even that. He needed a pacemaker, but that problem was complicated by a platelet deficiency—a bad combination. Keeping the pacemaker going to regulate the pumping of the heart would eventually result in excessive, incurable bleeding. He would slowly hemorrhage to death. John the physician knew exactly what was happening. Even as he tried to take brief versions of his old walks and outings, he made plans. He started getting his own letters and papers together. He sold a vintage imported car he had kept running since the early 1960s to a younger physician he knew to be a discerning and appreciative fellow enthusiast. He tried to get outside, pause, chat with people he knew, reflect.

Within two weeks of getting the pacemaker, he was gone. Everybody rallied: the family, the town, the university, the medical community. The leave-taking and funeral were all done with dispatch and dignity. He was cremated. At the memorial service, his wife made sure there was minimum sentimentalism and piety, no soul-butter business, what Samuel Clemens would have called "tears and flapdoodle." The thing most people would remember from the service was the song that replaced a final hymn: "America the Beautiful." The priest wasn't big on the idea, but John's wife had insisted. It was, she said, the one thing he had asked for.

When the family started going through the personal effects, they found two letters from 1945. On official V-mail paper, they had never been addressed and had never been posted. They showed just how bad it had been for John in the Ardennes and afterward during what America had come to call the Good War. Written in third person, they were the letters of a young twenty-something looking down at himself or, in some cases, on the army and the whole damn bloody terrifying world. Accordingly, they spoke, in their furiously scribbled and scratched-out way, a sense of angry melodrama, reminiscent of the young Stephen Crane; but they also had a similar sense of strange detachment, a merciless, disturbing scorn. One letter opened with scorching indictment of anyone who might welcome him home someday as a returned warrior. "So I'm a hero, eh?" he began. "If they only knew." The rest of the long missive described the utter, disabling, trouser-wetting terror he had undergone, shivering and cowering in a hole, waiting out the interminable artillery, trying foolishly to bargain with God. The other letter, recounting his attempt at happiness during a stay at a rest and recreation center in Belgium, revealed how stupid and unappealing he had found army life. It had been base, mundane, sordid, and, worst of all, boring. Two letters, lying there all these years, lay bare the true education of a soldier. Out of the experience of combat, in survivorship, and even in some moments, perhaps, the small triumph of will over inaction, a soldier remembers with a strange shame the blind, unreasoning fear; out of all the rest, a soldier recalls the experience of everyday military life as the basest sort of quotidian tedium.

Somehow the tall, loping boy had redeemed all of this as well as his paternal legacy. His was a story to be reckoned with, and I was bestowed with the prize of knowing it because John was my friend. We were neighbors, yard and garden buddies who shared conversation and jokes, old anecdotes and funny stories. We were ex-GIs who—as they used to put it in the nineteenth century, when you could get scared going to Barnum's circus—had been to see the elephant. We were writers. We were husbands; we were parents.

I loved John, and I think he loved me back. He had no son. Since age twelve, I had had no father—my own was dead of the form of suicide in post-1945 America called work: a quick, nasty coronary occlusion, in front of my sister and me one Tuesday night in the TV room; before that travel, tension, coffee, cigarettes, and obsessive, twenty-four hours a day, three hundred sixty-five days a year commitment to a career, providing for his family, as a food chemist and company director. At some points our stories diverged. My father was too old for World War II, married and already a parent. He also held a draft-exempt status for his work, in charge of technical operations for a fruit-processing company. That was a certified wartime "essential occupation" if there ever was one. Boys from the county actually told stories about seeing cases of their applesauce cast up on the beach at Normandy. Still, growing up, I sometimes wondered how he felt about that, surrounded by slightly younger friends, relatives, and fellow workers who had survived, as we all vividly knew, Ploiesti, New Caledonia, Schweinfurt, St. Vith.

Not that he hadn't given me my own kind of father-story—one that had been plenty, I had come to believe over my life, for any son to live down. He had simply had the good manners to die, I was fond of saying, while he was still a saint—uniformly and truly beloved; as genuinely good a man, insofar as I could discern, as everybody said he was; the kind of father any boy ought to be proud to remember as an inspiration and example.

It was at this point that John's story and mine began to dovetail. In my youth I had been a flutist and saxophonist. I had been studious and unathletic, a benchwarmer in basketball, at the end of high school a lean whippet of a quarter-miler who had found some small satisfaction in a few senior-year wins over poor competition. Still, I was an odd boy whose oddity, I knew, was frequently chalked up to the fact that I had lost my father. I finished high school; I went to college; I wound up in the army.

Buried in that last fact was the great, secret bond between John and me: one of which we talked sometimes, freely and comfortably, albeit not often—just when one or the other of us felt moved to bring it up. The bond was this: when we were young men, we had both been in the kind of war you don't write home about—the scared shitless, I'll do anything if You (even though I don't believe in Your sorry ass) get me out of this war; and the bored-to-death stupidity and inanity of general life-in-the-military war that surrounds it and smothers it in bland ugliness. Twenty-five years after John's time in the Ardennes, I had known both things while doing a year in the armored cavalry in Vietnam. I came out of it with a head full of bad dreams and an urgent desire to make something of a life, for whatever reasons. Unlike John, however, I took forever to even begin to get there. I went back to a high-powered graduate school and finished a doctorate. I got a job writing and teaching at a big research university. I lived the life of a privileged academic, performing in the lecture hall and seminar room, traveling to big conferences and symposia in exciting places, impressing myself with some warmed-over romantic rationalization that it was my soldier's pay, my reward as the survivor's life. I drank and adventured, behaving meanly, selfishly, hurtfully. I broke relationships and drained the emotions of people who cared about me. Eventually, I found help. I married someone who loved me so much that I finally learned I could love someone back. We had a daughter. We bought a house in a neighborhood where I found a friend, also the father of daughters.

The rest of the story is the one I have tried to tell here. Make of the juxtapositions what you will. Make of the lost fathers and left-behind sons what you will; or the attempt to look behind the myth of the Good

War; or of the degree to which, for many of us, whether we went to war or not, the example of the Greatest Generation will always reduce us to a sense of our personal ingloriousness. It's there for the taking. I will take the friendship, from the man who taught me how he had redeemed the fear and boredom that had almost ended things for him in that hole in the Ardennes. The part about making a good life is still up to me.

An Old GI Looks at Generation Kill

"No lie, GI," as we used to say in the 199th Light Infantry Brigade near Xuan Loc back in the late 1960s. "There it is." If those sentences do not seem to say much now, neither did they speak to anyone outside the world of combat back then. Then *or* now, the only people we ever thought worth saying them to were ourselves and one another.

I wonder whom the current generation of American combat soldiers will find to talk to besides one another when they come home, not to mention decades hence. Given the way our government currently recruits its armed forces—an allegedly volunteer military but in many respects just a product of conscription by other means—I anticipate that they will, in a way perhaps even beyond the vast draftee armies of earlier eras, mainly have just one another. For, like us before them, several years into a dirty, murderous, increasingly unpopular war that people would just as soon forget, they are already history, in that particular way Americans are so very good at making things history: as in, "oh, yeah, but that's history." What can an old GI like me do to call attention to what has happened to them, to commemorate their experience as soldiers in a particular war in a particular place? We can at least honor them by trying to get some things about their experience on the record, if only on a page of memory somewhere, to be found by some future antiquarian.

More than four years into the Iraq War and even longer into continuing warfare in Afghanistan, what do most Americans at home know about soldier life out on what John Ellis has called the "sharp end of combat"? Not much, as far as I can tell. How much do most Americans want to know? Save for the families, friends, and loved ones of soldiers—and combat veterans of earlier American wars like myself who think about them every single day—probably even less. Well, we all need to know what it looks like, to get behind the slogans and clichés on the right and the left. We need to see that, for all the talk about "boots on the ground," the experience of close combat today does not look remotely like MTV-style television ads for the new action army or marines. Concurrently we need to know that, for all our ideological conceits on the left or right, "Iraq" is not Arabic for Vietnam or El Salvador, or anything else one might care to put on a bumper sticker or in a fancy editorial—although, to Hollywood's credit, a place that looks like Mogadishu, Somalia, in *Black Hawk Down* might be a candidate.

As the war on the ground is practiced in Iraq or Afghanistan, this is what we need to know about it: it can be fatal for those going out and doing it every day, a frightening and deadly form of combat combining the worst terrors of anti-insurgent operations with the meat-grinder relentlessness of the great wars of attrition. Actually, it's worse. Philip Caputo, in his superb memoir of service as a marine lieutenant in Vietnam, identified accurately the particular sources of savagery in that conflict—its signature combination of guerrilla action with civil war. To this may now be added age-old religious hatred.

And this is why we need to know: we have sent enormous numbers of our young men and women off to fight in this war for several years now and will be sending them off to fight for even more years in the foreseeable future. Further, those numbers will soon include vastly increased proportions of our younger citizenry. Until now, we might have bought a vehicle insignia or a T-shirt reading "We Support Our Troops," knowing deep down inside that it's just code for "Just As Long As It's Not My Kid." There's no time like the present to stop kidding ourselves about that. For months, army and marine recruiters have not been making their quotas. As of this writing, the overall death toll of American combatants is moving steadily toward three thousand; the number of wounded now exceeds twenty thousand, with large numbers of those surviving massive injuries from which even a decade ago they would have died on the battlefield. One hundred fifty thousand or so is the figure usually cited for forces deployed in the major war zones in Iraq and Afghanistan at any given time. The latter number may be of some comfort to those who remember five hundred thousand plus in-country at the height of the Vietnamese conflict or the million-plus armies of World War II. But the important figure is how many people are cycled in and out. There is a simple measure for this: current soldiers in the combat zone are already in the middle of second and third tours and facing more. What will we do when the next phase breaks out, or when North Korea or Iran brandishes nuclear weaponry, even if not to use against us or our allies but to sell to our enemies? No one is mouthing "draft" yet, but that is where the soldiers will have to be found.

We need to know what we are demanding of the people currently deployed and those who will replace them. Indeed, we need to start thinking right now of the cost that combat service in the wars of this new century will exact on this and future generations we send to fight for us in the long terrorist twilight of a world that ended for all Americans on 11 September 2001.

At the moment, what does this war look like for the Americans daily going out to engage the enemy in one of the traditional combat arms— infantry, armor, armored cavalry, artillery, engineers, military police— or in myriad combat support branches—transportation, quartermaster, ordnance, signal, intelligence, civil affairs? What do our young men and young women in uniform experience inside the news clips of the big orange explosion, the plume of smoke, the cacophony of rocket and automatic weapons fire, and then the aftermath of dust, sirens, flashing lights, and security people waving away news cameras? What will be the last thing they see? Or, if they survive, what will they bring home in their memories, stowaways from that small world of combat–of shooting or blowing up people only a few yards away or risking a similar fate at the hands of such people; of having to put their hands on the wounded and the dead; of getting ready to get up and do it all over again?

Aside from the infrequent brigade- or battalion-sized operation, on the ground in Iraq the combat action is mainly at the level of the company, the platoon, or the squad-size detachment–not just for the army but for all service branches. The basic mission is the patrol–also known as search and clear, reconnaissance in force, and ground reconnaissance. The object at its most bald and aggressive is to find the enemy, close with the enemy, engage the enemy through fire and maneuver, and destroy the enemy. This used to be called search and destroy. In this war it can be as important to disrupt the enemy, dislodge the enemy, put the enemy to flight, interrogate those who may have given aid and comfort to the enemy, and seize enemy arms, supplies, and intelligence materials left behind. A lot of combat work in the current war is preemptive: the sweep or security mission, the police raid, the encircling and cordoning off a designated area. Some of it is notably static, particularly in populated areas: manning and guarding the strongpoint, the checkpoint, the control point. At night there is a lot of bunker-manning. Compared to Vietnam, there does not seem to be a lot of ambushing and virtually no use of isolated, three- or four-man observation posts or listening posts. What used to be called night defensive positions–although there are still plenty of hasty perimeters drawn at the end of a given day's operations–tend to be large and well established, with guard post and bunker systems of some permanence and sophistication. To put it bluntly, the general combat drill in this awful and terrifying war seems to be that everyone pretty much goes home at night, and the war more or less shuts down: Iraqis wait out the everyday carnage in their houses and hideouts in towns and cities, and Americans wait in their compounds. The odds seem fairly long even on getting rocketed or mortared at night, although it certainly appears in casualty reports. The fortified American installations tend to be bigger than what Vietnam veterans would remember as firebases, but for the most part they are less elaborately developed than the large and sprawling enclaves of Da Nang, Bien Hoa, and Long Binh. They are not likely to be overrun, but they are also not replete with comforts staggering in their difference from the animal misery of life in the field. The air force manages to do it up right, with a place called Balad Air Base in Iraq—billed as the second-busiest landing strip in the world after Heathrow and nestling the predictable post exchanges with wall-to-wall electronics, a miniature golf course, bountiful mess hall cuisine, and, failing that, a Popeye's, Pizza Hut, Subway, and Burger King. But army and marine facilities are generally not so representative of American culture as air bases. One surmises that this difference is a function of de-termined adjustments in head-to-tail ratio between combat and support forces, with the army and marines having a lower proportion of support forces. A salutary result of that statistical quirk seems to have been the erasing of distinctions between soldiers with their asses in the grass and REMFs—rear-echelon motherfuckers, as we used to say in Vietnam.

Part of this disposition is a matter of terrain. Iraq has no jungle or tropical forest, no triple-canopy bush or thick, dripping canal and rice-paddy vegetation growing right up to the perimeter wire. The topo-graphic maps are not wall-to-wall green, their dense contour lines con-cealing wall after wall of impassable brush and slick, tangled, muddy ravines. The dominant ground of this war is desert: not exactly sand, but more like dusty, broken clay. Along the river systems are canals and marshes. And in northern Iraq and Afghanistan, units operate across vast expanses of barren mountains.

The new arena of combat is also defined, of course, by where the en-emy chooses to operate. That is especially true given the relative small-ness of the overall force deployed—roughly one hundred and fifty thou-sand troops, as opposed to the half million in Vietnam—compared to the geographical expanse and the challenge of the theater of operations. For instance, American troops have not seen mountain fighting since the 1951–53 period of bloody stalemates in Korea. The main difference between previous counterinsurgency operations and current ones, however, particularly in Iraq, is that small-unit action now entails a lot of urban warfare. U.S. troops have done this kind of fighting before: during World War II in Europe or the Philippines, during the Korean War in Seoul and Pusan, and even during the Vietnam War in Hue, Saigon, and elsewhere as part of the Tet Offensive. The difference now seems to be a constant challenge of fighting and staying alive amid the deep, forbidding, channelized spaces of street and building, wall and intersection, the strange light-and-shadow midworld of combat in the dust and rubble.

This work is done, as always, on foot. The new development in this war is how troops get there to do the work. As opposed to Vietnam, especially, where every image or memory seems to include wall-to-wall helicopters, everyone in this war, including infantry moving quickly into close combat, seems most commonly to get where they are going in ground vehicles. For the soldier, there is still the abyss between covering large spaces of ground on wheels or in the air and then humping over a lot more of it on foot. Still, in what they call the warspace, the combat environment, one finds a lot of big ground machines: mostly Humvees; some Bradleys, the standard light-armor assault vehicle; the occasional M-1 Abrams tank. The Humvee is now the ubiquitous means by which even the infantry rides to its operations. In Vietnam the roads were packed with jeeps (quarter-ton), three-quarter-ton trucks, and five-ton trucks (in those days, because of their World War II ancestors, still called deuce-and-a-halfs); the air was dense with helicopters, the ubiquitous Hueys in all their myriad configurations – command-and-control, gunship, supply, and logistics, whole flights of troop-carrying slicks. Mixed in were LOACHes (light observation and reconnaissance helicopters), Cobra gunships, and big, sturdy, twin-rotor Chinooks.

The Humvee seems to be the Huey and just about everything else of the current war. Again, the technology comes in bewildering configurations, some official – cargo, recon, assault, infantry-carrying – some, especially with ad hoc armor designs, decidedly improvised. For someone like me, who spent his time as a platoon leader in a tracked armored cavalry assault vehicle (ACAV), and then as an executive officer, in a now-miniscule jeep running the red clay roads of Third Corps at constant full throttle, the Humvee seems a useful compromise. It is really big, fast, mobile, well-armed, and for the most part reasonably armored—but it also comes with its own problems. It is a big target, and in terms of the people and equipment aboard, lucrative for the enemy. In my war, maybe it is just a foolish illusion I harbored that once I got out of my tracked vehicle and into the now-vanished M-151 quarter-ton, people didn't usually mess with jeeps or individual cargo trucks. You could get sniped, though. If the problem involved mines or booby traps, in a jeep or truck you also had the small solace of knowing that the end would be quick, with not much of you left. The problem with Humvees is that they're big enough to help you survive but still small or vulnerable enough for you to be seriously injured. To a civilian, an urban Hummer looks enormous compared to the other vehicles on the interstate, but a fully loaded military Humvee is claustrophobic inside. The soldier riding in the turret ring and manning a weapon is going to catch it from automatic weapons, a rocket-propelled grenade (RPG), or any kind of roadside bomb or improvised explosive device (IED). The others down inside, driving and firing out the windows, given the penetrating power of the RPG and the enormous blast power of most mines or roadside bombs, become fast-moving fugitives from the law of averages. It must be terrible riding into combat that way—likewise with the Bradley.

If troops are brought in by helicopter and lifted out the same way (what Vietnam army commanders called insertion and extraction), the catastrophic costs of high-tech combat in the rubble can be similarly exacted—as was evidenced more than ten years ago in Mogadishu—on a moment's notice; except now the main aircraft is the big, sophisticated Black Hawk, getting support from the complex and expensive Apache. When either of those goes down, it's a very big deal (as will be seen, keeping such craft airworthy is also a major enterprise in southwestern Asia). For cargo, one frequently sees the old, sturdy Chinook helicopter. There's still an odd Cobra out there in its navy or marine paint and gunship configuration. But almost vestigial, generally speaking, seem to be the big airmobile lifts depending on helicopter units the way almost everything in Vietnam depended on helicopters.

Part of the reason, of course, is that the military enemy, unlike the Vietcong and North Vietnamese army, aren't out there somewhere beyond the firebases and the cities; or if they are, there's virtually nothing but endless space for them to evaporate into—and, according to reports particularly chilling to any Vietnam veteran, tunnel complexes. The emphasis on wheels rather than blades, one suspects, may have much to do with the sand. How it impedes function of individual- and crew-served weapons is a constant headache, but this must be small change compared with the way sand grinds, abrades, and clogs everything from blade and rotor parts to turbine engines and filters. One imagines the same problem with tactical jet aircraft, even the old F-4 Phantoms and the low, slow, ugly Warthogs that acquired a troop- and tank-killing reputation in the first Gulf War. In Vietnam, the sky seemed to be alive with machines and weaponry twenty-four hours a day: helicopters, jets, forward air controllers zipping around in fast little propeller planes, and medium bombers lumbering in on call. One remembers the sky, day or night, as a vast orchestration of thump, bump, rattle, boom, aircraft of all descriptions dropping bombs and spewing tracers, rockets, flares, red streams of aerial automatic cannon, an arc-light B-52 strike going in somewhere over near Cambodia; and then one remembers all of that mixed up with around-the-clock artillery, marking rounds, fire support missions, defensive concentrations, harassment and interdiction. In Iraq that is largely missing too. Because of its low latitude, Vietnam is really dark at night. For soldiers in the field, the darkness was accentuated by the jungle and, in the wet season, by incessant rain—a downpour, a drizzle, maybe just a steady drip, drip, drip. In Iraq, the unbroken silence everywhere must make the darkness even seem darker. A generator suddenly shutting off must sound like the end of the world.

Along with the infantry in Iraq, the other combat and combat-support arms go hurtling out of the compound through a kind of instant reality-warp into their own versions of this strange, savage war just outside the gates. In mechanized units, the Vietnam veteran will see in Iraq the occasional ACAV, the old M-113 armored cavalry assault vehicle mounted up with a .50-caliber machine gun to the front and two 7.62s — firing the old, roughly .30-caliber, NATO round—one on either side of the back hatch. The most common form of light armor is the Bradley, part infantry track and part assault carrier, and actually developed in two corresponding models—the M2A3 for mechanized infantry and the M3A3 armored cavalry version. Officially known as the Bradley Fighting Vehicle System, it mounts a twenty-five-millimeter cannon, a TOW missile launcher, and an advanced 7.62-caliber machine gun in addition to spectacular communications and sighting and target acquisition systems. Having gotten U.S. troops into the heart of Iraq in two lightning assaults, the Bradley is decidedly not another high-tech disaster as far as serviceability is concerned, as was the old M551 Sheridan. In current fighting, vulnerability is another story. The mine, the roadside bomb, the car bomb, and the simple, deadly RPG that remains every vehicle crewman's worst nightmare basically do to the Bradley what they do to the Humvee. The results are not reassuring. Bigger and safer but seen less frequently now is the tank that was so important early in the big-unit war fought against the Iraqi army, the M-1 Abrams. Then, now, and for years to come, as a main battle tank it is technologically superior to anything comparable in the world. In survivability it rates far better than a Humvee or a Bradley. The problem remains of close-in fighting, where it is still highly vulnerable to the armor-penetrating RPG—after all these years still the irregular fighter's cheapest, simplest, and most effective weapon, and present in Iraq and Afghanistan (as far as combat reports suggest) in terrifying, almost unstoppable abundance.

For troops on the ground, artillery is still there for crucial support and, as in Vietnam, is quick, accurate, and immediately on call. Missing, however, are the ubiquitous fire support bases, a battery here, a combined section or two there, comprising a set of vast grids of interlocking ranges and calibers. Like everything else in a support capacity, artillery battalions and brigades are massed on the big installations. On both ends of professional artillery combat as it is waged now, the new technologies of target identification, communications, and fire coordination are outstanding. Soldiers once hoped for a reasonably competent sergeant or lieutenant on the ground calling fire with a map, a compass, a fairly good sense of direction, a decent memory for terrain features, and a head for math good enough to understand grid coordinates, azimuths, and fire direction procedures, and a counterpart translating all the information simultaneously into the basics of a fire mission. Now, exact map coordinates come out of Global Positioning Systems, the little handheld GPS gizmos used by hunters and fishermen. Artillery fire direction centers haven't seen aiming circles or plotting boards in decades. Plenty of bad things can still go wrong, however. Accidents of war kill plenty of people, combatant and civilian alike. A bad adjustment call or a defective round can create holy hell when it lands. Getting everything absolutely right is still catastrophic when the target winds up full of bits and pieces of noncombatants. For these reasons, artillery operations in the new war zones now seem meager compared with Vietnam; most missions are devoted to direct support. Gone are all the marking rounds, automatic defcons, blocking fires. Particularly notable by their absence are the notorious H&Is (harassment and interdiction), largely random, immense expenditures of ammunition and firepower, with usually few results, save noncombatant casualties immensely benefiting the propaganda cause of the enemy.

Combat engineers get a lot of new work in this war. One of my students, married to an engineer lieutenant, recently called him a sapper. There's a word you haven't heard for a while. They still build and repair bridges and roads, erect and maintain fortifications and the like; but they also do a terrifying amount of what we used to call EOD (explosive ordnance demolition) work: defusing and blowing up IEDs; mapping and removing minefields; sweeping roads; in some cases they're back to almost medieval siege-work such as entrenching and clearing and mining old fortifications. Also in the forefront of combat operations now are large numbers of military police. I used to detest MPs in Vietnam, manning checkpoints and running around in their cool V-100 armored cars trying to give speeding tickets. With their shiny helmets, clean uniforms, neat brassards, they ranked right up there on the useless-asshole scale with the Vietnamese traffic cops, the White Mice. In the current war, MPs are taking a lot of the savage wounds and death from IEDs and car bombs, with the latter frequently manned by suicides at the wheel.

It must be utterly terrifying, with a truck or a sedan rushing at you while you try to match vehicle identification procedures and the rules of engagement, to run through the realization day after day that this is the last thing on earth you will probably see. A similar mindset must be part of the mission for every soldier in the support branches. The end of your life, at least as you know it, is waiting right out there on the street.

For a while, relatively novel military specializations got a large role in events. Suspicion of weapons of mass destruction (WMDs) fueled a big political controversy about going to war in the first place. Meanwhile, on the ground, the likelihood of finding even small amounts of chemical, biological, and perhaps radiological agents placed a big demand on the U.S. Army Chemical Corps. Similarly, as long as threats persist from other military powers in the region with helicopters, jets, and medium- to long-range missiles, major commitments will be required of air defense artillery units. For command and staff functions, there are still all the big command centers, what Vietnam GIs used to call the puzzle palaces. Although the housecats—as blazoned in recruitment spots—actually do now sit in front of computer screens, the combat effort still requires plenty of what used to be called Remington Raiders, clerks, and jerks. In vivid contrast, however, is the rest of the old REMF stuff— construction and maintenance of facilities, fuel and water supplies, food service, and waste disposal. It is virtually all licensed out to civilian contractors, most notably Halliburton. (And sometimes, as with the ubiquitous old RMK-BRJ construction-equipment days of Vietnam, only the acronyms have been scrambled: a major Halliburton subsidiary is still Kellogg, Brown, Root, for example.) What is newly ironic in the "outsourcing" market is that one finds similar arrangements for much of the old top-secret hunting and killing stuff. Among the military forces on the ground, however, one still finds a lot of special-operations people everywhere: Rangers, Green Berets, navy SEALs, marine Recon, and Delta Force. In Afghanistan, as evidenced by a June 2005 report on the deaths of a seventeen-member navy commando team in a single helicopter shootdown, after nearly four years of war, special-ops units still search areas of Pakistan for remnants of the Taliban and the elusive leadership of Al Qaida. In Iraq, special ops are mixed up with incredible numbers of civilian contractors—Blackwater USA is a notable brand name—working "security" for everyone from diplomats to war-zone wildcat entrepreneurs.

For everyone involved, from the most elite special-operations professional to the infantry private in the field, one finds a distinct uniformity in the basic killing tools: a suggestion, at least, that in contrast to much Vietnam weaponry, technology is on the individual soldier's side. Out at the sharp end, the infantry rifle is the light, strong, fully automatic M-4. Ironically, it still uses the works of an M-16, which thirty-five years ago was the best infantry weapon in the world provided—because of its refined mechanism—you didn't use it too much under combat conditions, moisture, mud, dirt, sand, dust, or you didn't try to fire it through a lot of vegetation because of the light, small-caliber, tumbling round. Apparently they finally got it right. As opposed to a limitless Vietnam substitute inventory of Browning Automatic Rifles (BARs, pronounced *B-A-Rz*), M-1s, M-2s, M-14s, CAR-15s, pump shotguns, one almost never sees anything in Iraq photos but M-4s. In Vietnam, I personally opted for an M-79 grenade launcher, a simple, single-shot area weapon we called a blooker. That one is now in a new configuration, packed on the bottom on a Star Wars–looking over-and-under arrangement, an M-4 rifle plus grenade launcher rechristened the M203. The old infantry squad and vehicle-mounted machine gun, the M60, firing the 7.62 mm NATO round, has been upgraded into the more effective M-240G. On the ground, the old M60 Vietnam "pig" has been altogether supplanted by a lighter infantry weapon, the M-249 SAW, an extremely light weapon with a high rate of fire, and using the same small-caliber 5.56 mm rounds as the M-4. Meanwhile, up there on the vehicles, and still going strong, is the pre–World War II .50-caliber machine gun. It can now alternate in the turret ring, however, with an automatic grenade launching system, the MK19.

Mobile communications have been refined and made operational at the individual-soldier level, involving both radio and cell phone technologies. As usual, much of it is capable of transmitting and receiving over enormous distances but fails when someone badly needs to speak to somebody else barely yards away. The night vision equipment is spectacular, lightweight, individual, and helmet- and weapons-mounted—as far beyond the old Vietnam starlight stuff as the starlight was beyond the old Korea and World War II infrared. The old flak jacket is now integrated into a system of body armor. The steel pot is now lightweight Kevlar, contoured to fit the ears and the back of the head. The old combat-helmet rules about avoiding ground concussion apparently have been superseded by common sense about the utility of chin straps. You can't boil water or shave in your helmet, but when you run or duck or dive it stays on your head.

For most units deployed, food now seems to involve nearly wall-to-wall hot chow. Soldiers of all ranks in nearly all operational conditions eat in enormous mess halls, like college and university student unions, with salad bars, appetizing desserts, and iced drinks (the comparison to college facilities is further reinforced by the availability of physical fitness facilities, gyms, workout rooms; computer centers, banks of monitors, keyboards, and printers). Virtually all the food-service work is subcontracted, including KP. In the field, troops get MREs (meals, ready-to-eat), just coming in when I was in Vietnam. We called them Lurp rations in those days because they were issued mainly to elite recon units (LRRP, or long-range reconnaissance patrol). Compared to the C-rations that preceded them, Lurps were absolute four-star combat chow—it sounds candyass to me, at least, to hear young people complain about MREs now. Still, the dishes don't sound appetizing: meatlike patties; spaghettis, stir-fries, stews, and goulash-type stuff. At least MREs come with their own little chemical heating units: just crush to heat. No need to hunt up the fuel tabs, which nobody used if they had a pinch of C-4 plastic explosive.

Coming out the other end, shit and piss still presumably go where they always have in the field: on the ground or in the nearest cathole. In forward areas as well it is still an army with the old pit latrines, rank, ammonia-smelling pisstubes, wooden three-hole shitters, some with cut-off fifty-gallon drums, so the refuse can be pulled out through trapdoors in the back, soaked in diesel fuel, and burned to dispose of it; but outside of combat zones in Iraq, chemical toilets prevail.

Combat-soldier amenities generally speaking seem often to have gone from just that primitive to just so currently sophisticated. Communication with home involves no airmail letters, muddy, sweat-smudged, with "free" scribbled in the postage stamp corner; no cassette tapes; no Mars calls, telephone patched in with radio. People call home on cell phones; they use e-mail and text messaging and shoot instant photos back and forth.

In cases of the worst message home, curiously, the casualty officers still drive up in military cars. For the families, the news arrives way ahead of the old telegrams. For the troops themselves, the news of the war or from back in the world is as close as TV monitors and websites, on laptops that double and triple as movie theaters, MTV monitors, and PlayStations. A large number of young U.S. soldiers entertain themselves with video games. Ironically, like the movies and many of the rock videos, many of the popular ones are R-rated. In the movies and videos the rating is for sex or profanity; in video games, it is more commonly for "graphic violence."

Somewhere around this point, an old GI becomes startled by all the other Vietnam War things the Iraq War is not. Because of the regular-tour policy, based on major-unit deployment, there is no R & R, a sudden week of civilian luxury at some exotic Asian or Pacific destination. Some thirty-five thousand troops a year, it is reported in the *New York Times Magazine*, get four-day facsimiles of an R & R pass at the comfortable facilities established at Camp As Sayliyah, located at Al Doha, Qatar, a U.S.-friendly principality jutting off into the Persian Gulf from Saudi Arabia. There, male and female, they may enjoy a Chili's restaurant, a Burger King, and an Orange Julius, workout facilities and swimming pools, a day spa offering haircuts, manicures, and pedicures. At an on-base hall, also not unlike some student unions, they can actually get beer and wine—three servings maximum. Intoxication and intercourse, as it was frequently styled by eager Vietnam GIs, this is definitely not. As to in-country stand-downs, because of shortness of operations in relation to return-to-base time, one no longer sees units limping back in, after a month or six weeks in the field, with fouled weapons, dysentery, jungle sores, and uniforms rotting off their backs. At base camps, one finds no seventy-two-hour orgies of instant oblivion, attempts to erase combat memories with beer and steaks, booze and pot, Filipino or Australian bands, and Okinawan or Vietnamese strippers. Because the Iraq and Afghanistan wars take place in Islamic countries, in the middle of a region where everything depends on keeping the good will of regional allies and impressing even regional enemies with our respect for Islamic religious strictures, there is no booze around, period. As opposed to Vietnam, where you could stick your hand through the wire and get anything from Cambodian Red to serious opium, the main drugs available to American troops in Iraq and Afghanistan seem to be tobacco, caffeinated beverages, and over-the-counter stimulants: it is not an untroubled, drug- and alcohol-free military body. But the war for American ranks is at least a war with no juicers and heads; no redneck EM clubs and black-power soul shacks. It is also a war without the constant sexual contact between American soldiers and local women that so pervaded the Vietnam War. There are no massage parlors; there are no short-time girls peddling themselves along with Saigon tea; there are no "indigenous females," as they used to call them, period. In the most bizarre way, with American military forces now full of women in places we would never have expected to see them—including bunkers and foxholes—outside the perimeter it is a completely womanless war. On the enemy side that also includes the military obverse. As opposed to the women fighters and political workers of Vietnamese Revolutionary Socialism, Afghan and Iraqi women play virtually no role in the enemy military effort, constrained as they are by strict Islamic tradition.

If nothing else, given the rigid sexual partitioning, rates for sexually transmitted diseases are negligible—a fact relatively unheard of in combat-zone armies since the beginning of history.

Battlefield medicine continues to reduce drastically the number of wounds that even a decade ago would have been fatal. Rapid evacuation out of country places victims of wounds, accident, and illnesses to advanced military hospital complexes in Europe and in the United States. The relative numbers tell the story: American soldiers killed now number around 3,000; the number with wounds is generally quoted at around 20,000. The ratio works out to 1.5 killed in action for every 8 to 10 wounded in action. For much of the twentieth century, a proportion of one killed to five returning wounded but alive was considered astonishingly good, so the reduction in the death rate is very much an occasion for hope among soldiers and their loved ones. Medical treatment now includes a major counseling component, both for the traumatically wounded and for their loved ones and families. Post-traumatic stress disorder work is built into every soldier's experience. Even with full-scale deployments, departure and return are accompanied by individual soldier and family counseling, decompression, readaptation.

All of the new technologies notwithstanding, for any American serving in Afghanistan and Iraq in a combat or combat support role, especially under the relentless pressure of multiple rotations, the bottom line is that danger for nearly everyone involved bears a daily, distinctly personal edge. In Vietnam the front was alleged to be everywhere, along with the imminent possibility of personal death or injury. In retrospect, however, that wasn't entirely true for everyone. Of eight million people estimated to have served in the Vietnam-era U.S. military, between three and four million did tours in-country. Further, common information about head-to-tail ratios between combat and support troops suggests—quite dismally—that perhaps as few as one-tenth of the U.S. military in the war zone actually served in the field as part of maneuver units in combat. A vast number of people may have been anxious about going outside the wire, but probably nothing much would have happened to them as long as they remained in populated areas. To paraphrase the historian Ronald Spector, Americans serving in Vietnam more or less knew that a good and safe place actually existed, and they knew that place to be "in the rear with the gear, the sergeant major, and the beer."

In contrast, those currently serving with American forces in Iraq or Afghanistan only have to go outside the perimeter to encounter death and wounding just up the block—as near as the Baghdad airport highway or the Mosul marketplace; not to mention the godforsaken Sunni triangle towns and in the northern desert for the marines, as usual, with less equipment and goodies and more shitty missions. And no one should mistake it. This war has been full of heavy marine combat. Early on the spotlight was on the U.S. Army 1st Cavalry Division, the 1st and 3rd Infantry, the 101st Airborne. In the months and years since, for anyone who knows U.S. military lore, the various other formations involved have comprised a roll call of the great American unit histories: the 2nd, 4th, 8th, 9th, 24th, 25th Infantry; the 10th Mountain; the 82nd and 173rd Airborne; the 2nd, 3rd, and 11th Armored Cavalry; the 1st and 2nd Armored; the 1st, 2nd, and 4th Marines. Most notable of late has been the activation of the of U.S. Army 42nd, or Rainbow Division, from World War I–a composite national guard unit, now a showpiece outfit for reserve and national guard combat operations.

And this may be yet another of the most important post–Vietnam War developments–perhaps one of the two or three defining features of combat soldiering in this war: the commitment of reserve and national guard troops as a massive proportion–reckoned initially at forty but now approaching fifty percent–of forces deployed at the outset. One need only look at the casualty lists. Interspersed among unit identifications such as the Third Infantry, Eleventh Armored Cavalry, or Second Marines are hosts of strange, unfamiliar numbers and designations, no-name reserve and guard companies and battalions from places like Royal Oak, Michigan, and Opelousas, Louisiana. And they have taken plenty of casualties, frequently recognizable as well by queer pairings of rank and age–a thirty-eight-year-old staff sergeant, a fifty-four-year-old warrant officer. Among them one reads the names of women. In official active-duty ground combat units, the MPs have generally been as close as women get. This has not been so in citizen-soldier support formations. A celebrated early casualty, PFC Jessica Lynch, was part of a national guard transportation unit that took a wrong turn into a town that the leading assault wave had not completely cleared. Killed that day was her best friend, also a woman. Of the nearly 3,000 American dead in Iraq, between thirty-five and forty have been women. Of the approximately 20,000 wounded, women have numbered between 250 and 300. When they have done the work of combat, they have rated decoration, as did a member of a Kentucky National Guard unit who recently received the Silver Star. It is one of the great shames of this war that women combat participants have been reduced, at least for the present, to being famous for their Andy Warhol fifteen minutes in the media.

All the Americans fighting in Iraq and Afghanistan will also need to be remembered as charter members of Generation Kill: weekend warriors who never dreamed they would find themselves in close combat. Never in this part of the new century at least, as in the last part of the old, will the reserves and national guard be historically dishonored as havens for well-connected draft dodgers. On the other hand, the costs have been immense. Many of the soldiers have been older than those in earlier wars, out of shape, ill-equipped, and inadequately trained. As to community support for and identification with the soldiers, there has not been since World War II something as close to grassroots patriotism; concurrently, not since then have multiple combat deaths devastated a particular community or locality: an NCO and several enlisted soldiers killed in an ambush from a transportation unit housed at a county armory; nine members of a district marine reserve recon platoon going down in a helicopter.

Whatever the unit, in army and marine operations, day-to-day execution of duty and consistency of morale—as noted even by such critics of the war as General Barry McCaffrey—continue to distinguish most units currently deployed in active combat as consisting of the best soldiers we have ever put in the field: well trained, well disciplined, and highly professional—and now, on second or third tours, notably experienced. Particularly at the level of the maneuver unit, commanders and individual soldiers rewrite and adapt military doctrine to forms of combat evolving daily before their eyes. Although there is the eye-catching controversy of the friendly fire mishap such as that involving former professional football star Pat Tillman, who left a multimillion-dollar contract to serve as an enlisted man in the Army Rangers, one does not get the sense of good American soldiers, as in *Apocalypse Now* or *Black Hawk Down,* being hung out to dry as part of some feckless captain's or ticket-punching lieutenant colonel's counterinsurgency on-the-job training. Nor, save with the Abu Ghraib prisoner abuses by a poorly trained national guard MP unit, or a much-reported refusal by a group of reservists to do continued convoy duty without proper security, do we hear much about totally unprepared or defective second-line units.

To put this more simply, U.S. forces in Afghanistan and Iraq are performing as professionals in every sense of the term. They are frequently deemed so by virtue of being all-volunteer—although debate continues on whether, in the traditional active-duty units, they are really that, or, more likely, just exceptionally intelligent, physically fit young people who couldn't find good jobs or who needed money to go to college. There can be no doubt that professionalism, albeit at whatever cost, has been maintained—as it was definitely not in Vietnam—by regular troop rotations, deployments in and out by units rather than tour-of-duty assignments for individual soldiers. In the Vietnam War, unless you were a career professional—a lifer, as they were called in those days—the tour in-country was 365 days; or for the marines, always adding one for bad luck, thirteen months. One day into the tour there, a soldier was an instant short-timer, ready to go out at least a day sooner than some FNG (fucking new guy) coming in. This certainly still happens in the Afghanistan and Iraq conflicts within a unit as people are lost to wounds, death, illness, expiration of enlistments, and the like, and others are brought in to replace individuals. But mainly there is a strong attempt to maintain cohort identity and integrity. In this respect, it does seem probably less lonely a war than the FNG/short-timer war famous from Vietnam books and movies.

On the other hand, against the salutary emphasis on unit deployments, cohesion, refitting, retraining, and rotation, the effects of such policies on the lives of individual serving soldiers have driven the army and marines down to the point where virtually no active-duty formations remain untouched as a reserve. At present, the army and marines are even running out of reserve units. We have used our soldiers up.

Soldiers in enlisted grades such as private first class, lance corporal, or corporal dominate the casualty lists, sometimes as many as ten a day in small forces. Our forces are often hopelessly outmanned and outnumbered by 130,000 insurgents and warring factions. Where will we get more soldiers to fight and maintain security? Why did it take us this long to figure out we would need to do that? At times the army has not met recruitment quotas. In one instance, it first fudged the quota and then missed *that* number by twenty-five percent. In May 2005 the *New York Times* reported that fewer than half the trainee slots were filled at the five major U.S. Army training facilities. By the end of that year, 80,000 newly trained soldiers were projected as necessary for commitment to active duty. It is altogether too late for a draft.

Equally dire, in this case with a pronounced mirroring of Vietnam-era mismanagement, is the attrition of noncommissioned officers of all ranks. As squad- and section-level leaders, even young, relatively low-ranking sergeants are operating as military professionals with energy, expertise, and experience. Seasoned senior noncommissioned officers have now also profited from ten to fifteen years in grade. No one is talking yet about repeating Vietnam-era shake-and-bakes—bright enlistees rushed through OCS-style NCO academies to fill ranks that by the third year or so of the conflict have been depleted of old-timers going on their second or third wars—but that time might come. Again, the casualty lists tell the story, along with the records of unit rotations. Professional NCO leadership is probably the most crucial personnel issue now facing combat formations, as soldiers of such rank and experience cycle out or are lost to wounds, death, illness, age, and decisions to leave the army (not unlike those now being made by many one-term enlistees). One can hear, speaking from beyond the grave, Bernard Fall, who essentially wrote the book on the American war in Vietnam before we fought it. In an epigraph his book on the French military disaster at Dien Bien Phu, *Hell in a Very Small Place,* he invokes the Israeli strategist Menachem Begin, commenting on his country's insurgency struggle against the British. "When an empire is in decline," Begin is quoted as saying, "it sacrifices its non-commissioned officers."

Commissioned leadership from platoon and company rank all the way up to field grade and general officers may well be the best the United States has ever put in the field. To be sure, one finds the occasional saluting cuckoo, careerist, or martinet, the bane of armies throughout history. But generally officers seem motivated, smart, physically fit, professionally schooled, and frequently experienced on their way through the ranks with service in Airborne, Ranger, and other first-line combat formations. If you see field-grade command and staff people at the battalion and brigade levels in Iraq, they aren't flying around in a Huey and playing squad leader in the sky, as they were frequently forced to in

Vietnam. They are on the ground, wearing standard combat gear and bearing the usual coat of dust. You can tell that the talking-head general officers on TV have been primed, but they also show they know the script in a way that makes them sound appropriately gung-ho but also cerebral and executive. And there seem to be jillions of them. There does not seem to be a lot of ticket-punching, however. If the army or marines get a good officer in charge of a platoon, a company, a battalion, a brigade, or a division, they don't rotate him out. The officer leaves when the unit leaves. And that unit will be replaced with a new unit with new leaders.

A lot of leadership is needed to deal with who this enemy is and how they fight. We usually hear the terms "insurgents" or "ruthless terrorists" as opposed to "guerrillas" or "irregular fighters." Thus far, the vein of old racial epithets is mostly gone—gooks, dinks, slants, slopes, zipperheads; or of disparaging references to the enemy, such as Victor Charlie, Charles, Chuck, or Old Clyde. The preferred term so far as any exists seems to be Haji—Arabic for pilgrim, as in one who undertakes the Haj. There are no urban legends, as there were in Vietnam about the famous booby-trapped kid or the camp barber in the concertina war. Anybody now in the field needs no legends, anyhow, to contemplate an enemy who is that ideologically determined and, if necessary, suicidally brave.

The problem in this war is that the operative tactic is suicide itself. It's one thing to deal with revolutionaries who are willing to die for the sake of the revolution. It's another to know that every person you encounter may well be someone who has come out that day with the express intention of committing suicide and, if possible, taking you and as many other people as possible with him. In Iraq they suicidally come hurtling at you in cars and trucks, sit or stand patiently by the road, or walk into a crowd until they get next to you, and then blooie. Or they run around in the open trying to shoot at you in a bizarre, full awareness that you are going to shoot them down. In addition, we have long surrendered the erroneous theory that these people are hopeless third-world nihilists with a death wish or credulous kids convinced they are going straight to paradise with seventy-three virgins. No, they are soldiers whose idea of defeating a military enemy is to make it cease its occupation of Islamic lands by making the world pay—enemies, infidels, and believers alike—the price in endless blood and carnage.

The inventory of novel ways to die in Iraq spawns a new litany of terminologies and phrases: suicide bombs, car bombs, roadside bombs, IEDs. American technology can't develop fast enough to keep pace with cottage-industry ingenuities. Jamming devices designed to counteract cell phones and garage-door openers used as detonators fail to register as new infrared signals. Improved blast armor on vehicles proves inadequate against buried shape-charge weapons designed to penetrate particular points of vulnerability. On Baghdad lots, car-bomb specialists now outsource their work to motorists who unwittingly buy vehicles already packed with plastic explosive. For Vietnam War veterans, some of the most common ways to get blown up, shot, or incinerated have a dread familiarity. Anyone who spent time in an ACAV or a Sheridan remembers the day he saw one hit a mine big enough to lift the whole thing right off the ground and then bring it back down in a crumpled, burning chunk. The enemy automatic rifle of choice is the old, reliable AK-47. And then there is the RPG: after all these years, there is still no more terrifying weapon in the world for the infantryman or vehicle crew than the rocket-propelled grenade. The acronym doesn't do it justice: a basic shaped-charge warhead with a tailpiece and a set of fins, originally designed as an antitank weapon, it becomes a lethal grenade only after it has done its job as an armor-piercing projectile. Sturdy, simple, easy to carry, assemble, and operate, it is reasonably accurate and incredibly destructive. If it hits you, you are vaporized. If it has to go through another surface first, it will blow off whatever part of you it hits next. If it comes at you through a wall, you will die from rocks, chips, concrete, or other debris. If it comes through the hull of a vehicle, you will be hit by molten metal and spalt flying around inside. Along with its own blast and flash burns, it will ignite any ammunition. It is absolutely the worst; and a six-year-old can operate it. Any Vietnam vet can tell you: what an RPG does to a human body is not worth bagging.

This is the bottom line. If you are wounded or die in Iraq, it is likely because you have been ambushed at very close range by an enemy with

AK-47s and RPGs, been shot by a sniper, been mangled by a booby-trap, or been blown up by some kind of very big explosive device. If none of these things happens to you on this tour of duty, you will wait in dread for them to happen on the next or the next after that. That is what the future looks like for you as a member of Generation Kill.

In the meantime, what can an old GI wish for you? Tight buddies and smart, resolute, humane officers and NCOs. First-class weapons, ammunition, and equipment. Good food, and plenty of it. Something cold to drink when you're hot and something hot to drink when you're cold. A dry, temperate, quiet, relatively safe place to get some sleep. Oh, yes, and not having to burn shit.

Squad Leaders in the Sky

"What is your situation?" Or,

   "Where is your flank security?" *"How many bunkers can you
see?"* *"Why aren't you moving?"*

   "Get off my fucking frequency." Or,

   *"You land that goddamn helicopter and get your ass down here on
the ground with me, and I'll show you exactly where my flank security
is,"* *"... how many bunkers I see,"* *"... why I'm not moving."*

This imaginary exchange will surely bring back memories for veterans
of the Vietnam War who tried to function as small-unit commanders
on the ground. Amid the daily work of war—in any situation from a

difficult point-to-point movement to a serious engagement with automatic weapons and rocket-propelled grenade rounds going off all over the place – there would come that call on your command radio net. The questions are the ones you heard every time. The responses probably never happened, or at least not in the form stated. They were the things you *wish* you'd said but didn't.

That voice in the air, sudden and godlike, feathered by helicopter vibrations: it had to do with a singular aspect of command and control in Vietnam that frequently drove a fatal wedge between platoon- and company-level combat officers – tired, hot, dirty lieutenants and captains out humping the bush – and the majors, lieutenant colonels, and colonels in clean fatigues orbiting above them in a helicopter with mapboards and grease pencils. We had a name for the problem. We called it "the squad leader in the sky."

For those of us who experienced the ground war of the combat platoons and companies in Vietnam – most of us now in our fifties and sixties – it's hard to imagine that our battalion and brigade commanders from those days are nearly all, if they are still alive, well into their seventies and eighties. As we remember ourselves from our late teens and twenties, they will always be in their thirties and forties, vigorous, imposing, and sometimes inspirational figures of authority and leadership. Majors, lieutenant colonels, and colonels – many of them veterans of earlier wars or of previous Vietnam tours during the advisory period – they were once the presiding deities of the world of close combat, with immense powers of decision making and life-and-death responsibility. They had charge of every immediate aspect of our existence: our food, clothing, shelter, health, morale. On their decisions rested our motivations and our fears; our safety and our danger; our diseases, our wounds, and possibly our deaths. They made the plans and gave the orders that sent us into battle. They were the ones we called on for reinforcements or support. They decided when sometimes we had had enough. If we were junior officers, they had the duty of overseeing our performance, assessing our leadership, writing our officer efficiency reports if we survived, and writing letters of condolence to our families if we didn't.

From the good ones – and there were those certainly meriting the phrase—we would have accepted orders to march ourselves and our platoons and companies through a brick wall if that is what they said was necessary. I remember getting a mission briefing one day about three months into my tour from a battalion operations officer I admired, a sharp young major, probably in his early thirties—the kind of officer David Hackworth would have called a romping, stomping combat stud. This one finished up by calling me a hard charger. And he knew exactly what he was doing: I was his boy from there on out. But I also remember other officers, many of them frustrated with being stuck in rear-area administrative jobs while they marked time for command slots—or otherwise getting their tickets punched, as it was called in those days, in various staff assignments—who we found contemptible for their pettiness and chickenshit. A few were just plain incompetent, if not downright dangerous, getting us into situations that even a PFC or second lieutenant knew were totally insane.

A handful went on quickly from what might be called Vietnam-era combat middle-management to general officer rank, with a few making ascent to positions of national visibility, influence, and decision-making power. One most prominent at the time, General Alexander Haig, vaulted himself overnight from mid-1960s Vietnam battalion and brigade command with the First Infantry Division (where he was awarded the nation's second-highest decoration for valor, the Distinguished Service Cross) to four-star rank and major defense and national security positions, including Watergate-era chief of staff in the Nixon White House, supreme allied commander of NATO forces, Europe, and, during the presidency of Ronald Reagan, secretary of state.

Two others ascending to the highest rank, more familiar to Americans today, were Generals Norman Schwarzkopf and Colin Powell—the first regaled in the popular imagination as Stormin' Norman, the inspirational commander of coalition forces leading them to lightning victory during the Persian Gulf War, and the other as the dignified, articulate, mediagenic chairman of the Joint Chiefs of Staff, and later, in President George W. Bush's first term, U.S. secretary of state. Ironically, it should be added, both made their way to the top in spite of second, midlevel tours in Vietnam—following earlier assignments as advisors to the army of the Republic of Vietnam (ARVN)—with the ill-starred Americal Division, enshrined in history as the parent unit of the troops involved in the civilian mass killings at My Lai. Schwarzkopf would command a battalion late in the war, taking over a unit in which discipline was virtually nonexistent, casualties were frequently a result of don't-give-a-shit carelessness, and morale was also in the toilet. Attempting to bring the unit back up to late-war combat effectiveness in the field while instilling enough discipline and self-confidence to make sure most of them got home earned Schwarzkopf the sobriquet Colonel Nazi. As if this were not likely to kill a career, he also achieved inauspicious literary depiction in C. D. B. Bryan's *Friendly Fire*, the widely read account of a mother's attempt to get the true story about of the death of a her son, killed by errant U.S. artillery. Colin Powell, a highly regarded major fresh from finishing second in his graduating class at the U.S. Army Command and General Staff College, was assigned as an American battalion executive officer at the beginning of his second Vietnam tour. His survival of the middle command echelon during the breakdown of the late-Vietnam army was nearly as fortuitous. Plucked from that position by a division commander who had read in the *Army Times* about his recent staff college ranking, Powell was vaulted to the staff position of Division S-3, or operations officer, usually a senior lieutenant colonel's slot. During this tour, as reported in his autobiography, Powell turned out to be the division staff member who led investigators to combat log entries from a year earlier confirming the My Lai incident and its cover-up. Meanwhile, while flying on a command and control mission, he earned the Soldier's Medal, the army's highest noncombat decoration for bravery, for pulling his division commander out of a wrecked helicopter.

A number of the other high-level commanders in the first Iraq War might be said to have been there largely by surviving various midcareer Vietnam assignments. Lieutenant Generals Calvin Waller (American deputy commander under Schwarzkopf) and John Yeosock, in charge of American ground forces, had done late MACV (Military Assistance Command, Vietnam) advisory tours. Lieutenant Gary Luck, commanding the 18th Airborne Corps, had followed an early Special Forces assignment with helicopter flight training and a second tour as an aviation officer. A fellow corps commander, Lieutenant General Fred Franks, as a major in the Eleventh Armored Cavalry, had left part of a leg on the battlefield during the 1970 Cambodian Invasion. (In contrast, virtually all the younger division commanders serving directly under them – generals including Thomas Rhames, 1st Infantry; John Tilelli, 1st Air Cavalry; Binford Peay, 101st Airborne; Paul Funk, 1st Armored; and Barry McCaffrey, 24th Infantry – were significantly pointed out as having acquired *their* basic combat experience and military philosophy by serving as platoon leaders and company commanders in Vietnam. And so would be the case with other top army leaders throughout the 1990s: Wesley Clark, Head of NATO peacekeeping forces in Bosnia; Tommy Franks, commander of U.S. combat forces in Afghanistan and Iraq; and U.S. Army Chiefs of Staff Hugh Shelton, Tommy Franks, and Eric Shinseki were all spotlighted as having made their early reputations in the Vietnam War as small-unit commanders.)

The vast majority of middle-ranking army commanders in Vietnam did not make general, retiring as lieutenant colonels and colonels. Further, it may be posited that a substantial proportion of them found themselves disqualified for further professional advancement precisely because of what happened to them and their units during their battalion and brigade command tours in Vietnam. As career soldiers at the peak of their professional development, they had spent decades getting ready for their great test of senior leadership on the battlefield, the one faced by generations of their distinguished forebears on their way to general officer rank: the command of a combat battalion or brigade. Instead, to borrow Stephen Crane's phrasing about Henry Fleming's fears concerning his reputation among his fellows, they wound up "a slang phrase."

What happened? It wasn't supposed to be this way. To be sure, nobody expected the old Frank Lovejoy scene, in midcombat, with some steady junior officer getting a surprise set of oak leaves pinned on his collar by the regimental commander. "What the . . . !" he protests. "The battalion's yours, Smitty," the colonel replies. "You've earned it." This was not an army or a war in which any realistic professional could expect to get "their" battalion or brigade by being pulled up from the ranks and then leading it for the duration. More likely, after World War II and Korea, Cold War duty assignments, or advisory missions to Asia, the Pacific, the Middle East, South America, or Europe, they had hung in there during the long march from junior officer to field-grade rank— major, lieutenant colonel, and in some rare instances colonel. There had been years of sitting on the Korean DMZ; patrolling the East German border or screening the Fulda Gap; going through the army educational system as well as completing graduate degrees in history, political science, international relations; in peacetime unit assignments, passing big inspections and getting graded on endless maneuvers and field training exercises; between deployments taking their families from post to post, doing the round of base schools, officer housing, and commanders' wives clubs.

Everything they did professionally they suddenly saw as possibly culminating in the actual grasp, in war, in Vietnam, of the holy grail of midlevel officership: the command of a battalion or a brigade in close combat. Eventually came the lumbering mechanics of finally getting there: the coveted Vietnam orders to join one of the big combat divisions or separate brigades; once there, as many as six months in some off-the-wall assignment waiting for a command position; then six months, tops, in command—at best, lifted out just about the time they figured out what they were doing, if not relieved early for not cutting it in some way, maybe pissing off some brigade or assistant division commander, or just getting nosed out for the next career officer standing in line; sometimes a couple more months in another shit job in the rear; then going home, for the vast majority of them all hope of promotion beyond colonel permanently gone, beginning to work on retirement or early separation.

It probably comes as little solace now; but if, within the officer corps, battalion and brigade command in Vietnam would prove so uniformly a disaster waiting to happen for many of its most able and dedicated career professionals, one can now firmly assert that many of the reasons were beyond their control before they got there, built into the nature of the army and the war. Chief among these was the structure of command itself, with its increasingly managerial model of military leadership. Midlevel officers found themselves placed in the position of plant directors, project managers, regional sales supervisors, told in an era of quantification, statistical modeling, process analysis, and rational management-by-objective to motivate their workers to go out and produce. So in the terms of command policy and authority, they found themselves trapped between the wars of the Washington planners and MACV/U.S. Army Vietnam generals and the wars of unit deployment and maneuver on the ground. But in the latter case they found the disconnect most pronounced. Here, the distance between the management model and the task of management itself could not have been more vast. As professional combat leaders they fell into the tactical abyss between the war of the big rear installations and main bases, and the small-unit war of the jungle, rice field, highlands. And it was here that most of them met the problem that broke their careers and often their souls. For the chief difficulty of battalion or brigade command in Vietnam, as seems to have been known to every small-unit officer and NCO soldier on the ground, was that there was no rational way to exercise such unit control, in the traditional fashion, from the ground up. To put this more concretely, aside from the rare battalion or brigade sweep, or the joint force or combined arms operation, virtually no direct battlefield leadership in tactical engagement in Vietnam ever rose above the level of company command. If anything, most of the fire-and-maneuver activity and decision making occurred not at the level of the company but at that of the platoon, the squad, the fire team, even the observation post or listening post, two or three people in a hole. It was a war of the micromission—the patrol, the ambush, the night defensive position, the short, intense firefight. Wounds and death came quickly and usually by surprise, one here, three there, another five somewhere else; they came from the hit-and-run attack, some quick mortar rounds, a sniper, maybe just a booby trap, the whole business done in a minute. Lieutenants and captains spent their days and nights in the field, sharing the misery, fear, frustration, and confusion of jungle combat, frequently separated on the ground from major portions of their units. Command was completely decentralized, with decision-making responsibility, judgment, and power lodged squarely in the roles of twenty-five-year-old captains, twenty-one-year-old lieutenants, eighteen- and

nineteen-year-old instant NCOs. Battalion- and brigade-level commanders found themselves in turn strange, hybrid, "combat" functionaries,
mainly prisoners of the shadowy midworld of the forward firebase; the
sandbagged tactical operations center; and above all—in every sense—
the helicopter, described aptly by one of their number as both "boon and
bane." Nervously distanced from the war of the generals, staff officers,
and assorted ambitious rivals and sycophants at the big rear-area divi-
sional bases and command headquarters, by the very nature of ground
combat, they found themselves nervously separated in much the same
fashion from the nine hundred or so soldiers in the field for whose literal
lives and deaths they were supposed to be directly—that is to say, by the
very code of the battlefield they themselves had learned as captains and
lieutenants—both professionally and personally responsible. Sitting in
forward tactical operations centers—or, more likely, flying to the scene
of the action, getting stacked below senior commanders doing likewise,
they somehow had to find ways of being useful to—calming, advising, in-
forming—fragmented elements of their command on the ground; doing
spotter missions and coordinating indirect fire, artillery, gunships, jet
airstrikes; relaying radio communications to higher headquarters—all
while trying not to meddle, complicate, micromanage. The fact of the
matter was that in many such instances midlevel command was just such
a complication for many officers on the ground—a nuisance, a bother,
sometimes the last thing you needed when somebody was shooting at
you. At the very least—or so it was easy to imagine for someone fighting
on the ground—it became hard to respect somebody barking combat
commands to you while wearing starched fatigues and spit-shined boots
and orbiting above the battlefield in a helicopter at a safe distance of
fifteen hundred feet. Battalion and brigade commanders in Vietnam,
in short, became the helicopter and firebase equivalents of the dugout
"warriors" so reviled in earlier conflicts.

On the account of the vast detachment from the war and sheer
creature comforts soldiers of all ranks saw being enjoyed by the po-
tentates of the big installations, the literature is replete—generals living
in air-conditioned trailers; graveled walks and flower beds tended by
enlisted aides; white-tablecloth headquarters dining, cocktails, wine at

dinner; lordly senior commanders holding court over after-dinner bad-inage, surrounded by staff (Schwarzkopf recalls being aghast at finding out that a junior officer in the Americal general's mess was responsible for composing a poem of the day); ceremonious briefings, spit-and-polish officer presenters, shined-up enlisted men snapping pointers on maps with acetate overlays; post-briefing palace intrigues, with staff rivals sniping to get the general's favor. Even as relatively high-ranking officers themselves, new field-grade commanders must have wondered how their role models and inspirational leaders from World War II and Korea could have forgotten midlevel troop duty with their own combat battalions and brigades. William Westmoreland had risen through the ranks of artillery command fighting in Tunisia, Sicily, France, and Germany, and making three combat jumps. Creighton Abrams famously had ridden the first tank into Bastogne. Frederick Weyand had spent World War II in Burma and China and had commanded a regiment in Korea. Bruce Palmer, Willard Pearson, James Hollingsworth, William Dupuy, Julian Ewell, John Tolson, Melvin Zais, and others in their earlier careers were well-known combat unit leaders. Now they all dwelt luxuriously in stateside bases like Long Binh, Cu Chi, Chu Lai, surrounded by incredibly bloated staffs, careerists, ticket-punchers, paper pushers jostling to be the next in command of a brigade or a battalion deemed to be underperforming under its current commander. Standing above it all, they prodded their minions toward competition for body count, inflated reporting, unnecessary endangerment of companies and platoons, elbowing and pleading for helicopter companies to conduct big airmobiles.

The dreadful pageantry of this remains memorably depicted in an early novel of the war, *The Lionheads*, by Josiah Bunting, a West Point career officer. The central character is just such an embattled middle-management figure, in this case a brigade commander, a colonel, nicknamed "Shuffling" George Robertson. Intelligent, cerebral, ironic, he reads Trollope while flying point to point in his command-and-control helicopter, basically trying to invent tactical doctrine for a composite, experimental unit, of navy riverine craft deploying army infantrymen in the delta. In the competition among brigade commanders for the favor of the division commander, Major General George Simpson Lemming, helicopters have not been deemed as essential to their mission as to that of the other conventional three-battalion brigades doing fairly standard airmobile search and destroy. As a result, Robertson's brigade is flagging in body count. At length he consents to a disastrous mission he knows to be wrong. At the end of the novel, his career is over and he knows it; and maybe he just doesn't care anymore.

Nor did such jostling and elbowing go on just in novels and movies. In the My Lai massacre Task Force Barker, the umbrella unit for the ground forces doing the killing, was an ad hoc formation, commanded by a hotshot lieutenant colonel. He was a favorite of the Americal Division commander, Major General Samuel Koster, basically given his own command. The actual battalion commander of the companies involved that day was elsewhere, basically in charge of his headquarters troops. So, in the personal narratives of highly decorated combat soldiers of midlevel officer rank, regarded among the best and most experienced tactical unit operations combat commanders in the army, we see careers and reputations ruined—frequently because of their disagreements with division higher-ups or resistance to policies dictated from Saigon. David Hackworth, Anthony Herbert, and John Paul Vann, all former enlisted men, found themselves insubordinate and eventually cashiered, largely over conflicts with ticket-punching rivals bucking for general. Likewise, Schwarzkopf recounts the demise of his brigade commander during the second Vietnam tour, Colonel Joe Clemmons, as a captain in Korea the real-life hero of Pork Chop Hill. While hectoring Schwarzkopf to get his battalion in shape after the tenure of a weak predecessor, he also stands up for him against an ambitious assistant division commander, a careerist one-star trying to score points with his two-star superior. It is a career-ending display of loyalty, with Clemmons shortly forced out of the army and retired a colonel.

But the worst part of being the perpetual men-in-the-middle, without doubt, was on the other side, in the role of actual battlefield leadership. At what John Ellis calls "the sharp end" of combat, a professional crisis became an ethical catastrophe. Again, the print literature does not lie, abounding with caricatures of the heliborne micromanager, the field marshal of the firefight—a reminder that clichés become clichés frequently by being true in the first place. In David Maraniss's *They Marched into Sunlight*—an account of the 1967 virtual annihilation of a battalion from the First Infantry Division in an enemy ambush—a forward air operations officer recalls nearly all attempts he saw at command participation from above in events on the ground below as generally possessing "the earmarks of a Chinese fire drill." So, as recorded in Ron Spector's *After Tet*, another officer recalled the specifics of a similar disaster as viewed from his own position on the ground. "The company I was a platoon leader with was engaged and taking some casualties, pretty big fight, and the battalion commander was almost forced off the air, and the brigade commander was on the net controlling one of the platoons, the division commander was talking to the company commander. All this was going on, and the company commander was getting pretty frustrated. He couldn't even talk to his own platoons because everybody was on the net." Indeed, as cited in one postwar analysis, the situation was so common as to generate a kind of nightmare fantasy. "We always had a horror," wrote one officer, "that one day things would come to a standstill. Overhead would be circling our battalion commander. Above him would be his brigade commander. Higher than both would be the division commander and hovering over him would be his corps commander. All circling in their 'charlie-charlie' choppers, all demanding to know what was going on down on the ground. So much command and control would be present that those with their 'ass in the grass' would no longer be able to function at all. It never happened, but it came close."

But it was still no fantasy. That fact is corroborated in a number of surprisingly frank accounts by officers caught in such command gridlock that they finally resorted to open insubordination as their only way out. Sometimes, as it turned out, if a presiding officer on the scene had some sense, he could jump in and back the ground commander. On other occasions, competing authorities would actually land their helicopters and have it out. In still others, conflicts begun over the airwaves—as depicted vividly both in David Hackworth's *About Face*, a military autobiography of the man called by Creighton Abrams "the best battalion commander in the army," and again in *Steel My Soldiers' Hearts*, a combat memoir of his final tour of Vietnam command—would extend into career-ending vendettas engineered by those who had found their authority challenged in the skies above the battlefield.

Officers in positions of substantial authority were not unaware of the problem, either, in some cases working out solutions. One senior officer, interviewed during the 1980s for a U.S. Army War College oral history project, had to struggle, he said, as an incoming battalion commander in 1969 to win the reversal of a standing unit policy requiring combat officers of his rank not to join their units on the ground. Fortunately, he found his appeal rapidly seconded by the brigade and division commanders. Still, he had to admit that luck was with him. His brigade commander happened to be Hank "Gunfighter" Emerson, one of the few airmobile officers known for his ability to work directly and expertly with troops on the ground. The division commander was Julian Ewell, whose career was anchored in World War II battalion command. Another officer noted his realization upon taking command that the lowliest platoon leader in the division on any given day generally found himself required to exercise something close to "field-marshal" authority on the ground. In response, he proposed a concrete regimen of pretraining, a filtering down of command independence where company commanders would be directly charged with educating their subordinates as individual decision makers and independent battlefield leaders. In his own practice, that officer wrote the following.

> When my company commanders have a contact, naturally they
> report to me but assuming I have it available, I'll switch a radio to
> their company command net and listen. I may be in a helicopter,
> however, I don't usually have one that much. I'm usually in a track
> or back here in the TOC [tactical operations center]. I usually put a
> radio on their net and listen and monitor. I listen so that I know what
> they told their platoon leaders to do and I know what action they're
> taking. I get into the act from the standpoint of informing them I
> plan to request a light-fire team, "can you use it?" I even contact
> "do you need my initials" etc. in order to get artillery on target and
> get air clearance, GVN [Government of Vietnam] clearances, U.S.

clearances to fire on a certain target. This is part of the Rules of Engagement.

I try to get in to offer him assistance where he needs it and then he knows I'm there. He knows I'm listening on his company net, he knows I'm also on the battalion net. If he needs me for help, he can call. If he doesn't need me but he needs some other asset, he knows that I can get it for him quicker than he can get it for himself. He can run his show. When he gets in trouble and he needs help in the form of another company, or a scout platoon, or anything of this nature he just lets me know.

Then I make every attempt number one to keep from screaming and hollering over the net because I don't think you gain a thing and it gets me so mad to listen to other people do it that I become very much aware of it myself and try to make sure I don't do anything like that. Let him run his own show and then his platoon leaders and his platoon sergeants, and his men know that he's running his own show and they don't have to have a battalion commander there in order to be successful. That they don't have to have a brigade commander or an assistant division commander hovering over them in their helicopter in order for them to achieve success. They've done it on their own and they're very proud of their own accomplishments. They are very proud that the artillery was called for and adjusted by their FOs right there in the ground with them, a young lieutenant or a sergeant or in one case a company I had it was a Spec. 4. They are very proud. That's one of their own, they live with him, they sleep with him, they eat with him and they know that this guy can deliver for them and that's what makes them, successful.

The reason he could rise to this level of thoughtfulness, he added, had much to do with his good luck to be in a unit where such command relationships seemed to be the norm, enforced by steady practice:

I feel most fortunate because I know there are other brigades and there are other divisions where a one-star general or full colonel telling squads and platoons where to go and they bypass the whole chain of command, feel they've really done a tremendous job when they get back and in reality have usurped the prerogatives of the company commander and the battalion commander and have destroyed, in effect, their confidence in their own capabilities. Likewise, with my company commanders, I think I can best portray this by example.

The above report has been quoted at length. The reason is simple: even to this day, it remains a model of what should or could have happened. In most cases, however, according to extensive interviews with younger field-grade officers about their experiences in Vietnam as company commanders – all of them selectees, it should be added, for the U.S. Army War College, and therefore hardly thwarted or aggrieved in their career prospects – it was exactly what *didn't happen.* Rather, respondent after respondent noted "the over-tendency of general officers to be squad leaders"; "interference by higher headquarters" and "the terrible syndrome of senior commanders"; "the fifteen-hundred-foot mentality"; "the guy up in the helicopter" with "nothing else to do but talk on the radio." As notably, even many of those who did not suffer from the problem addressed it specifically, if only to record their relieved exception in being assigned to a unit relatively unafflicted.

One went so far as to base his career-level War College Staff Study on the problem. The title he gave it made his view clear: "Maneuver Company Commanders and Their Battalion Commanders in Vietnam: No Shared Value." And he laid the details right on the line. Battalion commanders virtually never spent a night in the field or participated in daytime ground operations. They faked enemy body counts and wrote themselves up for phony medals. They directed squad operations from their tactical operations centers and persistently broke into communications during firefights. "By failing to share hardships," the author concluded, "to trust, to communicate, to provide vision, to subordinate personal ambition, to be visible and approachable, and to exude dignity and integrity, some battalion commanders impeded rather than contributed to successful combat operations."

The author was attempting to describe not simply the breakdown of command and control – a tactical failure. He was also describing what many troop leaders on the ground saw as a complete breach of professional and ethical faith—a failure, in the fullest sense, at least as the military defines it, of character: the willingness to share hardship and danger; the dedication to leadership by example; the ability to sacrifice; the acceptance of command with a commitment to making sure that when one left it would be with the conviction that one had done one's professional best.

To be sure, not every battalion or brigade commander could have ever been a Hackworth or a Clemmons. But there were also plenty of them who fit the definition of character described above and did their best to live up to it. Nor was there spectacle enough attached to their eventual retirements to require recording in a book. Some of them were forced out. Some of them just decided to leave. When a war winds down, there is always an RIF, a reduction in force. This war was no different. And as military professionals, they knew that was part of the contract. Most of them simply mustered out when the time came for them to go and slipped quietly and uncomplainingly into retirement and obscurity, carrying with them their frustration and sadness at a bad end. From field-grade base quarters they moved to tract houses in the suburbs or to little places in the country. Pensions were usually augmented by work at state jobs or in local government, in part-time businesses as a consultant or a planner, maybe service as the executive of a nonprofit. Some did charity work; some went back to school. Some chose to spend their final decades near familiar places like College Station, Texas, Charleston, South Carolina, or Lexington, Virginia, where they had been cadets; or near Fort Benning, Georgia, Fort Knox, Kentucky, or Fort Sill, Oklahoma, where they had taken their basic and career courses; or Fort Leavenworth, Kansas, or Carlisle Barracks, Pennsylvania, where they had gone to the U.S. Army Command and General Staff Course or the Army War College. Some retired to places near the big duty posts, with their post exchanges, officers' clubs, golf courses, and medical facilities: the airborne at Fort Bragg, North Carolina, or Fort Campbell, Kentucky; tankers at Fort Hood, Texas; aviators at Fort Rucker, Alabama; or just good places out west like Fort Carson, Colorado, or Fort Lewis, Washington. Many elected someplace warm where they could fish or play golf. Others went back to the bedroom suburbs around Washington DC that they got used to during tours at the Pentagon. In such places they read in the local papers the obituaries of their fellow soldiers, not many to begin with, but now, after three and more decades, one or two a week.

Over the years, how they must wince when they see themselves depicted, perhaps most famously, by the quintessential Vietnam colonel, the mad heliborne commander, Lieutenant Colonel Kilgore, played by Robert Duvall in *Apocalypse Now*, with his big First Air Cavalry patch and his garish blue cavalry hat, cranking up an airmobile assault on a coastal village so he can watch a championship surfer who has accidentally appeared on the scene, dealing out death cards on Vietnamese corpses, enjoying beer and steaks around a big campfire on the beach, a 1960s guitar songfest. "I love the smell of napalm in the morning," he exclaims. "It reminds me of . . . of . . . victory." Or there is the other mad colonel in the movie, Kurtz, the West Point– and Harvard-educated renegade Green Beret, alone in his jungle imperium. It was common knowledge that Kurtz was a fictionalized Colonel Robert Rheault, commander of the Fifth Special Forces, indicted with his officers for the Green Beret Murders. When the phrase "terminate with extreme prejudice" came up during the three-star, air-conditioned trailer lunch where Kurtz's assassin, Captain Willard, played by Martin Sheen, gets his orders from the general, played by G. D. Spradling, and the boy-wonder staff colonel played by Harrison Ford, the words were those of their own dishonored fellow officer.

In exactly this context, the directorial cameo of Oliver Stone in *Platoon*, renowned as the great film of the grunt war, is a rich joke. A former enlisted infantryman, Stone briefly appears near the end of the movie as a major–the only officer above the rank of captain depicted in the movie. He is seen giving instructions to a group of subordinates at a hastily erected firebase. When the base is overrun that night, he and his staff, comfortably underground and manning their radios, are blown away by a screaming enemy soldier who carries a satchel charge into their command bunker.

In movies generally, the only alternative to the lunatic played by Robert Duvall turns out to be the other extreme: Mel Gibson toughing it out as the heroic ground battalion commander of *We Were Soldiers*, iron-ically about the real First Air Cavalry and the Battle of the Ia Drang, the first large-scale engagement of U.S. infantry units with the North Viet-namese regular army. The steady, brave, resolute, no-nonsense profes-sional played by Gibson, airmobiled in with his troops at the beginning and lifted out only when the battle is concluded, is the real Lieutenant Colonel Hal Moore. He is further accompanied of course by the griz-zled, profane, warhorse command sergeant major, in this case the real Basil Plumley, played by Sam Elliot. In the real battle, Moore turned out to be the right man in the right place at the right time, a notably courageous and effective battalion commander, as did Plumley, a bat-talion sergeant major, and as did the vast majority of company officers, NCOs, and enlisted riflemen. On the other hand, there was another battalion in the Ia Drang campaign that isn't mentioned in the movie. With more than sixty percent of its soldiers killed or wounded, it suffered from a commander who lost control completely in the first minutes of action, remaining frozen on the ground and not in communication with a brigade commander overhead. The latter eventually had to land his helicopter and look for him while a major manned the radios. The fact remains also that Moore and Plumley simply beat the odds of getting shot down at any moment as part of a ground command group, includ-ing a captain wounded twice at close range by automatic weapons fire, the second time fatally.

For certain other figures well known throughout the Vietnam army, guts-and-glory flamboyance in the air *and* on the ground could actually seem to work in tandem. George S. Patton III, famed for his hands-on command of the Eleventh Armored Cavalry regiment in Vietnam, finished up as a major general. Legendary throughout the infantry, Hank Emerson, the "Gunfighter," with a battalion of the 101st Airborne and later a brigade of the Ninth Infantry, retired as a three-star. The dismal fact of the matter too often remained with cases such as that of Lieutenant Colonel Terry Allen, as recorded in David Maraniss's *They Marched into Sunlight*. The son of yet another famous World War II fighting general, and a battalion commander in his father's old division, he was hectored by immediate superiors into marching his command group along with his unit over difficult terrain in a major ground operation. In a massive ambush, he was shot down and killed at close range. His command was instantly beheaded; by the end of the day the battalion was reduced to clutches of survivors holding out in hope of relief.

This case defines the larger fact of the matter concerning helicopter command in the war generally—that it was frequently not just a legitimate but a necessary response to a central problem of leadership of battalion- and brigade-sized tactical ground combat units peculiar to the Vietnam War. (Further, it would now be foolish to blame the employment of a particular technology or tactical doctrine for the failure of command in a demoralized draftee army increasingly absent of experienced NCO leadership and riddled with drugs, racial strife, combat refusals, and fraggings of unpopular commanders; where the 365-day tour and the six-month command limit guaranteed perpetual combat inexperience against a skilled, confident, elusive enemy in some cases fighting over the same terrain for twenty years; where the characteristic mission of the latest ARVN fire-eater in the region remained search-and-avoid, and the preferred American helmet logo became a peace sign or FTA—Fuck the army.) Given the fragmentation of large-scale command, not to mention the difficulty of overland movement and coordination, it supplied the crucial ability to attend to subordinate units operating in combat in a timely and informed way. As opposed to World War II, to some degree Korea, certainly the war envisioned in training exercise after training exercise against Russian and Warsaw Pact troops flooding onto the central plains of Central Europe, Vietnam never in its most ambitious operations got near the big, traditional command extravaganzas of field grade and general officers on the ground advancing with their regiments and combat teams. Nor would it prefigure any of the wars that would follow—mainly big, quick, powerful, massively coordinated strikes, employing what would come to be called the Powell doctrine of "overwhelming force": Panama, Grenada, Afghanistan, Iraq 1 and, at least in the beginning, Iraq 2. In such wars, a favorite phrase would be "boots on the ground"; and in the vast majority of cases it would apply not just to general combat troop strength but also to the direct presence of upper-level troop leaders of all ranks. Vietnam, with its stunning variety of hostile terrain and its classical insurgency style of hit-and-run combat, impervious even to quick reaction force and massive firepower, would always be a sui generis war in many ways. Really the only practicable answer to problems of command and control above the platoon and company level – or so it seemed at the time – was the helicopter combined with the TOC (tactical operations center) system of instant radio communication. Battalion and brigade commanders were accordingly condemned by the nature of their tasks to remain essentially frustrated combatants. The war for them as troop leaders proved as bad as could be imagined; and the crux of their detachment and frustration was something about which the Career Course or the Command and General Staff College could teach them nothing. Individual good and brave men as they were, above the battlefield they were repeatedly forced to confront, in circumstances largely beyond their control, the inevitable failure of their own moral leadership in a job for which they had trained all their professional lives.

To put it simply, the vast majority of battalion and brigade commanders were well-trained, dedicated, hardworking professionals trying to do their job. In the main, they comprised anything but a parade of idiots, all needing to be shot down or otherwise unseated from their heliborne command post, subjected to company-commander and platoon-leader insubordination, relieved of command, sent home, retired from service. There were of course the clichés and caricatures: the ones who never left the tactical operations center; the ones who rode around and screamed at people returning from operations in scroungy uniforms; the ones who tried too hard to cultivate the reputations of being crazy bastards, jumping out of a helicopter running around and waving a .45, chasing down a Vietcong suspect in a bunker complex. But most of them were people who had not arrived at their command rank by accident; and, when entrusted to exercise the authority of that rank in combat, they were also people who tried to do their best for their troops and the army they loved. To this day it is hard not to feel their hurt and shame when they run into a reminder of what we thought of them or the nicknames we tagged them with.

Call them what you will now—maybe just the men in the middle. They were realists, or they wouldn't have gotten as far in the army as they already had. And in their consciousness of themselves as career military professionals, make no mistake: they were disposable, and they knew it. At the time, as now, military promotion was strictly a game of numbers once it approached the highest levels. And the numbers have never been encouraging. At the height of the Vietnam War there were 130 combat battalions in the field; there were 2,500 lieutenant colonels eligible to command them; there were seventy-five slots for infantry brigade commanders; there were two thousand colonels. To take this from the angle of a typical division, in 1969 the Twenty-fifth Infantry listed the following turnover rates—in this case reflecting actually a more or less "normal" rotation—for field-grade officers below the rank of major general: three assistant division commanders, six brigade commanders, twenty-two infantry battalion commanders, two tank battalion commanders, two armored cavalry squadron commanders, and eight artillery battalion commanders. This doesn't begin to count division staff officers, including vast numbers marking time—finished with their periods of command, waiting in the wings for a command slot to open up.

Afterward would come the selection for general. Then as now, anyone could do the numbers on that as well. No more than three to five percent of colonels made it. Ninety-five to ninety-seven didn't. That was the army. And they knew it. But they weren't ready to have to live down a war where they would be remembered as irrelevant, useless, a joke. Vanishing into the professional abyss is not too strong an image for what happened to them. Vietnam had made them somewhere between superfluous and negligible, and it would take the army a long time to make the breach in the command structure right again. Even in the mid-1980s, the recollections of a young lieutenant colonel about his experiences with small-unit command in Vietnam close to two decades earlier were telling. A midcareer Army War College selectee clearly on the fast track, with a bright career ahead of him, he would eventually retire with four stars. Still, he noted that, in his twenty-year army career to date, the greatest prestige he had thus far experienced attaching to any position was that of a captain commanding an infantry company in the 101st Airborne Division in Vietnam.

Nobody wanted it that way. The lieutenants and captains on the ground in Vietnam respected their seniors, wanted desperately to find them skilled, decisive, experienced, and inspirational as leaders, tough but supportive; they counted on them for support, advice, encouragement, wisdom, the occasional jacking-up in the name of professional education, the odd word of praise. The officers at the level of battalion and brigade command—at least most of the ones I knew—would have done nearly anything to lead from the ground, usually from the front. But it just wasn't that kind of war.

Still, there are plenty of people to remember. One junior major was so manifestly inspired as a leader that he'd commanded a battalion, being jumped over the heads of God-knows-how-many lieutenant colonels standing in line, and he eventually wound up in the same White House Fellows class as Colin Powell. He made it to three stars. A senior lieutenant colonel on his second tour of battalion command was already a hard-core legend from the First Division. He turned out to be as humane and decent as any officer I ever met. Hurt badly in a helicopter crash just before I left, he retired a colonel. On the other hand, there was also the one who had the bright idea of sending me overland with a platoon of tracked, noisy, diesel-breathing ACAVs to deliver dog food to the concealed position of his tracker team. And there was another who triumphantly gigged us on a command maintenance inspection, with all our tanks and ACAVs in the field, for having a slightly overfull oil level in one of the motor pool jeeps. The battalion commander I admired above all others, however, was the real deal: West Point, 1955; wise, profane, hilarious; a mission kind of guy if there ever was one; but somebody who also had that gift for being with the troops. Not a timid or officious or dipshit bone in his body. One night out near Gia Ray, my troop commander, a captain, was having trouble getting artillery during a blown ambush. He kept trying to work through the clearance system but kept getting put on hold. The problem had something to do with a colonel in charge of the ARVN advisors back in Xuan Loc. Suddenly, a voice came over the radio, as if out of nowhere, calling the artillery battery. "Shoot it," said the voice. "Initials, Juliet Whiskey Charlie." The initials were those of his name. He had been awake, monitoring it all. His troops were in danger. He called the mission, on his personal responsibility, and put his initials to it. It was just like him. He retired a colonel. He died late last year, out in College Station.

Where are the Juliet Whiskey Charlies today? Right there with their troops. Talk to any company-grade officers who've had combat duty in Afghanistan and Iraq and they'll tell you so. But soldiers don't get to choose their wars. In Desert Storm and the opening stages of the Afghan and Iraq 2 wars, battalion and brigade commanders got to charge inspirationally along with their units across the vast spaces of desert because the tactical situation allowed it. Today the insurgency war on the ground dictates a far more decentered command-and-control policy rather similar to that of the Vietnam War – a managerial attitude of vigilance and responsibility. Still, majors, lieutenant colonels, and colonels are largely out there with their troops, distinguishable from them in battle dress only by some small tab of rank, not surrounded by a large command group. They did not just get off a helicopter; they are not just about to get on one. They are probably in a Humvee or maybe in a mechanized unit, a Bradley. The chances are good that their tactical operations center is wherever they are. With advances in communications range and portability, they have pretty much everything they need right with them. That goes for the dedication as well. One would like to think that at least some of this has been bought for them by their predecessors in Vietnam, who were not nearly so fortunate to be in the right army in the right place at the right time – and yet in the majority of cases gave everything they had, including their careers and sometimes their lives. From their hard lessons in some degree has come the knowledge of today's battalion and brigade commanders that they are exactly where they need to be.

Home of the Infantry

If an election were held to choose the Holy City of the United States Army, my guess is that Columbus, Georgia, would be the top vote-getter. Columbus is the home of Fort Benning. Fort Benning is the home of the infantry. For anyone who knows something about American military history, the Infantry School at Fort Benning is the home of the modern U.S. Army. It is the place where, in the years after World War I, a forward-looking commandant named George Marshall, having served as the chief operations and plans officer of the American Expeditionary Force under General John J. Pershing, and thereby having learned the requirements of twentieth-century mass warfare, set up a curriculum to educate a new generation of officers in the complex demands of leadership, command and control, communications, planning and operations, supply, and logistics. It is where Marshall allegedly compiled his famous black book, which comprised, with few exceptions, a roster of officers passing under his observation and tutelage he marked for future positions of leadership at the highest levels of command authority. Along with Dwight Eisenhower and Mark Clark, he singled out Omar Bradley and Joseph J. Stilwell, who had served at Benning as instructors and developers of the infantry curriculum. Among students he identified younger leaders, including J. Lawton Collins, Matthew Ridgeway, and Maxwell Taylor. Later in the same period, Fort Benning became a center of training for parachute infantry warfare, the birthplace of new formations that evolved into the great World War II airborne divisions, the 82nd and the 101st. After World War II, the post became the permanent home of the airborne school, the ranger school, and the infantry officer basic and career courses. As famously depicted in the 2002 movie *We Were Soldiers*, to meet the new demands of post–World War II counterinsurgency warfare it became the birthplace of helicopter airmobility, with the experimental Eleventh Air Assault Division, eventually renamed and sent to Vietnam in 1965 as the First Air Cavalry. Later, additional units, including my own–the 199th Light Infantry Brigade, christened the Redcatchers and expressly configured and trained for operations in Vietnam–were also deployed from Fort Benning as part of the buildup of American forces and returned there to have their colors furled. In the decades following Vietnam, through operations in Grenada, Haiti, Panama, and elsewhere, Fort Benning gained prominence as home base of the Ranger Regiment and allied Special Operations units. And from the Persian Gulf War through current operations in Afghanistan and Iraq, it has served as the hub of training and deployment for combat operations. In its latest incarnation, according to a Department of the Army announcement, it will combine the functions of the Infantry Center with those of the Armor School, to be moved from its longtime location at Fort Knox, Kentucky, into the new Maneuver Center of Excellence at Benning.

As a combat veteran of the war in Vietnam, for me the Fort Benning–

Columbus complex holds two places of memory, albeit in jarring juxta-position—with one as hallowed and memory-laden as the other is strange and nearly surreal. The first is a memorial to a brigadier general killed in action with my unit in Vietnam. The other is a place of commerce where a former lieutenant, court-martialed and convicted of mass mur-der in Vietnam, has spent most of those same years as a prosperous businessman.

My place of great personal reflection is on the base at a building called Bradley Hall. Once the main hospital for the wounded return-ing from World War II and Korea, it is now the home of the National Infantry Museum, which depicts through displays, artifacts, and memo-rabilia the history of the U.S. Army foot soldier from the colonial wars to the present. There, the heart of memory for me is on the third floor, where a reception and reading area has been established in honor of Brigadier General William R. Bond, a former commander of the 199th Light Infantry Brigade and the only general officer killed by enemy fire on the ground in Vietnam. Presiding over the room is a handsome, well-executed portrait of the general, in jungle combat uniform.

It is certainly a good likeness. I was among the last people to see him alive, wearing just such a set of jungle fatigues and carrying a rifle around two o'clock on the afternoon of 1 April 1970. Shortly afterward, on a sweep of enemy ambush positions about a hundred and fifty feet from where I was standing, he was shot in the chest and killed. I re-member talking to him that day as if it were this afternoon. He had flown in, on his commander helicopter, to take charge of a battle that had been raging off and on all day. Several platoons from my unit had gotten pinned down in a big ambush, with a killing zone several hun-dred meters long, manned by a main-force Vietcong regiment in heavily fortified bunkers. An early morning artillery convoy had received the first attack. They had barely avoided being overrun and annihilated. As new forces rode into the battle area—an armored cavalry unit organic to the brigade, in which I served as executive officer—they too took heavy casualties, with tanks and armored personnel carriers burning all over the place. Although by noon the situation seemed to be stabilizing, by midafternoon nothing much had improved. Even after nonstop artillery, helicopter gunships, and jet airstrikes, it was a locked battle. During a break in the fire missions, the general decided to land. In retrospect, I know what he was trying to do: rally us, get us moving again, expand the perimeter and break out of the killing zone. Once on the ground he gave an order to make a dismounted sweep of the bunkers to our front. He joined the line of troops as they moved forward.

He came by the old infantrymen's ways through a career of carrying a rifle and leading. He was also proud and protective of all of us, in letters home calling us gallant. He was entitled to the archaism. Born in Portland, Maine, he went to college at the University of Maryland, where, after undergraduate study and a year of law school, he enlisted in the army. Rising quickly to the rank of staff sergeant, he was selected for OCS at Fort Knox. Commissioned as a second lieutenant, he was chosen for training with the new parachute infantry at Fort Benning. In 1942 he jumped into Sicily with the Eighty-second Airborne Division. He then volunteered for the Rangers, commanded by Colonel William Darby, and went ashore with them at Salerno. He went in again with the Rangers at Anzio, where he was wounded while fighting with the first regiment at Cisterna. Reduced from nine hundred to half its strength, the whole command was finally overrun. Too badly wounded to be taken out, he was made a prisoner of war and sent to a camp in Poland. As the German forces retreated in the east, he escaped and joined a Russian reconnaissance unit. When the end came, he was marching west across Europe toward the U.S. Army.

Between wars, he married Isabella Sedgwick, the daughter of William Ellery Sedgwick, editor of the *Atlantic Monthly*. He became something of an Asian specialist, serving with advisory missions in Korea and later in Thailand. He continued troop duty, including command of a brigade in the 101st Airborne. There he experienced a heart episode—a "tremor" it was called, some kind of palpitation or arrhythmia, resulting in his being disqualified on medical grounds for ground combat. Through boards and appeals, he sought and eventually won reinstatement. Promoted to brigadier general, after several tours in the Pentagon and at the age of fifty-one, he took command of the 199th Light Infantry. It's quite a story—almost something of a life of the century. He was in his third month of command when his life ended on a dusty road near Tanh Linh, Third Corps Tactical Zone, Vietnam—on a stretch the troops had already taken to calling ambush alley, in the kind of action we used to call the Battle of the Latest Trailbend.

The second outpost of memory, one might call it, for the Vietnam infantry soldier in the Fort Benning–Columbus complex, will seem at such variance from the first I have described, so bizarre, even surreal, as to represent a juxtaposition that, if it didn't already exist, would have to be dreamed up by some genius of absurd postmodern invention. Four or five miles away, at a major intersection of the interstate spur connecting Columbus with the main entrance to the post, the place of memory is the V. V. Vick Jewelry store in the Cross Country Plaza on Macon Road. There, the store manager, having come into a prosperous and success-ful career in the business through marriage with the founder's younger daughter, is a former U.S. Army lieutenant named William L. Calley. He is also the most notorious living war criminal and convicted mass mur-derer walking free in America. Fort Benning is the place where he trained as a soldier and later went through infantry OCS. It is also the place to which, after his participation in the 1968 My Lai massacre of more than four hundred unarmed Vietnamese civilian noncombatants, he was returned for trial, convicted, and sentenced to life imprisonment. He subsequently served out three and a half years on the post under house arrest until his sentence was commuted by President Richard Nixon.

For most Americans who remember My Lai as the signature event of the Vietnam War, Calley personifies the failure of American combat discipline and leadership. A junior-college dropout—remembered, if at all, in his premilitary drifting through a series of nondescript jobs, for his innocuousness—he had to be recycled through officers' training, barely making it the second time. A small, insecure man, in every way, es-pecially with the challenges of Vietnam, he found himself completely in over his head. Once commissioned, he was able to elicit no respect from those with whom he served. According to Wayne Greenhaw's biography of Calley, "Very few of the people who worked with him on a regular basis liked him." His commander in Vietnam, Captain Medina, was in the habit of calling him Lieutenant Shithead in front of his men and replying to him in conversation with the phrase, "Listen, Sweetheart. . . ." Soldiers in his platoon despised him as well. All in all, he seems to have been a classic of the short-man/short-fuse caricature of the petty martinet ubiquitous in military lore. In the field he was a terrible map reader, bad with a compass, and given to foolhardy tactical judgments. Angry and loud, he tried to mask his incompetence with noise and excitability. There was just "something about him," one soldier remarked, "that rubbed people the wrong way." His monstrous role at My Lai and removal from command may have saved his life. He was marked as a candidate for a fragging—that is, assassination by his own soldiers.

During his trial at Fort Benning, Calley got so much mail from the public that it was said he bought a thirty-five-dollar mechanical letter opener. When court was not in session, he spent his time with a journalist, John Sack, who conducted tape-recorded interviews for an as-told-to book. Calley got a celebrated visit and a formal, public expression of support from a friend in the neighboring jurisdiction just across the Chattahoochee River: Governor of Alabama George C. Wallace. Another journalist, Wayne Greenhaw, who took him home some weekends to Montgomery, Alabama, remembers him as oddly affectless, almost goofy. For a brief period he was allowed to make speeches to groups rallying in his support. Substantial fund-raising efforts were made in his behalf by a number of right-wing patriotic organizations.

After deliberating for more than ten days, the military jury found Calley guilty of premeditated murder of twenty-two villagers of My Lai. Before assessment of punishment by the jury, Calley was allowed to speak to them. "Yesterday you stripped me of all my honor," he said, with a kind of theatrical illogic; "please by your actions that you take here today, don't strip future soldiers of their honor—I beg you." After seven more hours of deliberation, the jury sentenced Calley to life at hard labor. Initially, he was transferred to the main U.S. military penitentiary at Fort Leavenworth, Kansas. On 1 April 1971, however, at the order of President Richard Nixon, he was released to await the outcome of his appeal. Within a few days he was returned to Fort Benning and placed under house arrest. A series of new legal actions followed, whereby his sentence was gradually reduced, first to twenty years and later to ten.

During the period of review, about three and a half years, Calley lived in bachelor officers' housing at Fort Benning, basically in what the military calls confinement to quarters. Meanwhile, in actions separate from those above, Calley advanced a February 1974 petition in federal district court for habeas corpus. When in September the court finally granted Calley's petition, it also essentially invalidated his 1971 conviction because of violations of his legal rights during the proceedings. The army appealed this decision to the U.S. Fifth Circuit Court and asked the presiding judge not to grant Calley's immediate release; the judge ordered a brief stay, but the full court upheld the release pending appeal. The matter played back and forth through a series of findings and counterfindings until Nixon once more intervened, commuting the sentence to time served. Calley was paroled in November 1974.

The dominant media image of Calley in these years projected him as kind of clueless, almost pathetic scapegoat. He was the only participant in the My Lai massacre ever convicted. The single other officer brought to trial, his immediate commander, Captain Medina, was acquitted. Medina's superior, Lieutenant Colonel Barker, was killed in Vietnam. A brigade commander was relieved. The division commander, Major General Samuel L. Koster, was removed from his post as commandant of West Point, demoted in rank, and retired.

Calley stayed in Columbus after his release, where his life took a turn for the better. He eventually married the daughter of V. V. Vick, a local jeweler with a reputation as a respectable, self-made businessman. Under his father-in-law Calley became a branch manager in a store the family had opened on Macon Road in 1969 in a new shopping center, the Cross Country Plaza. The Macon Road location, initially considered something of a risk, prospered under the management of son-in-law Calley, who was described in a 1983 article as its most popular salesclerk. When the downtown store closed, the Macon Road store became the family's main place of business.

When V. V. Vick died in 2006, an article in the Columbus paper summarized the life and career of this prominent, well-regarded citizen. A husband and father, a "conservative" business owner, a churchgoer, a member of civic organizations, he was said in the last twenty years mainly to have turned over the business to his son-in-law though he still came to the Macon Road store to visit with old friends. Mentioned at the end of the article were the marriages of Vick's two daughters, including that of Penny to William L. Calley. "Calley," the entry concluded, "was a former U.S. Army lieutenant court-martialed in 1971 [*sic*] My Lai massacre of 22 civilians in Vietnam. He now runs the Columbus store." A newspaper staff member tells me that the family didn't mind the marriage notice, but they thought the My Lai part had no place in the obituary. To them he was son-in-law Calley, a respected member of the family.

Citizen Calley. According to my newspaper acquaintance, over the years people got to thinking of him as the nice little salesman who helped Grandma pick out a wristwatch. At the same time he was always on the alert, disappearing into the back, frequently with the collusion of protective employees, when anybody who looked like a writer or reporter came sniffing around. The Calley home was on Hilton Avenue, in a residential district near the Columbus Country Club and not far from the store. Among acquaintances, William L. Calley Jr. reverted to his boyhood nickname, Rusty. Nonetheless, his son born in 1980 was named William Laws Calley III. The boy went by his middle name. When carpooling, Calley was just "Laws's daddy."

For all such apparent contentments, Calley was also known in the local bars as a heavy after-work drinker and big tipper. The newspaper staffer I spoke to said that the drinking was the sort that wasn't going to stop when he got home. He also said he had once actually confronted Calley in the store about his silence on My Lai. Calley gave him the impression, he said, of somebody who was well aware that he'd managed to manipulate the media into treating him like a celebrity recluse, and treating V. V. Vick Jewelers and the Hilton Avenue house like his sanctuaries.

V. V. Vick Jewelers constitutes a far more dismal space of Americana. It is tucked away in a nondescript, dying midtown shopping center. Empty stores on either side, it sits among a Subway sandwich shop, a

Chuck E. Cheese's Pizza, an Athlete's Foot shoe store, and a Books-a-Million. Sitting back in a dark corner, with its fake brickwork and carriage lanterns, from the outside it looks like a 1960s mausoleum. The windows display a sparse inventory laid out on sun-bleached draperies. Inside, the store is low-ceilinged, dark, almost cavernous, with a kind of antiseptic mortuary smell. Middle-aged women employees alternate between standing idly at a service desk and chatting around the table in a fitting area for rings. One sees no customers. The parking lot is mostly empty. As if obeying some final working out of the dramatic unities, Calley himself, after more than three decades, is now said to be gone, separated from his wife, no longer involved in the business, and living with his son in Atlanta.

Thus one can visit, within a few miles of each other, two quintessentially American places that speak the complex legacy of the Vietnam War. The National Infantry Museum – although a fund-raising campaign is under way to build new quarters – still occupies its home of three decades, on the edge of a large lawn called the Field of Sacrifice. Among monuments to units including the World War II Rangers, the First Infantry Division, and the First Air Cavalry, there is a recently erected memorial to the 199th Light Infantry Brigade, my brigade. Inside the museum, much of the Vietnam section of the exhibit is also centered on Redcatcher lore, including displays on a platoon sergeant who won the Distinguished Service Cross, a lieutenant who helped recapture the Phu To racetrack during the Tet Offensive, and a commanding general named Frederic Davison, the first African American to hold such a position with a major combat unit in Vietnam.

If you go up to the Bond Gallery in the museum, you'll find on the first landing a portrait of Benning, the Confederate general for whom the fort is named, and on the second, the founder of the Infantry School, George C. Marshall. Along the walls of the Bond Gallery are period paintings of George Thomas (the Rock of Chickamauga), William T. Sherman, Philip Sheridan, and others. As noted, the portrait of General Bond is the only likeness here of a general in combat fatigues. He wears a Vietnam-issue Redcatcher Patch, subdued green and black, with black embroidered stars on his collars; sewn above one pocket is a name tag,

"BOND," and above the other a standard one reading "U.S. Army." His sleeves are rolled regulation style: up to the elbow. His steel pot with its jungle camouflage cover rests on his knee.

For me the impression of all this, even after so many years, remains one of complete disconnect. The general seems to embody then and now everything that was great about the greatest generation. Ask anybody about what army units they've heard of, and they'll say the 82nd or 101st Airborne. Any Ranger today knows about Cisterna, the way every marine knows about Chesty Puller. Any Redcatcher knows who General Bond was, how he spent the last afternoon of his life, on the ground, in combat, against a large, heavily armed enemy force, with his soldiers. In contrast, Calley and his role in the actions that day in My Lai represent everything that was wrong about the Vietnam War: a lieutenant who never should have been an officer, paired with a derelict captain, who took orders unquestioningly from a cowboy task-force leader; a new, insecure, completely inexperienced brigade commander who stood by while the task-force leader took his instructions directly from a fast-track major general. On the ground, a completely undisciplined handful of squads and individual soldiers acted out the bloody rage of a frustrated and demoralized division. And make no mistake: they murdered, raped, sodomized, and mutilated. Over four hundred Vietnamese were slaughtered. It was every bit as bad as history tells us it was.

What was left for me to do or see in Columbus to make sense of any of this? Around noon, some kind of strange, magnetic attraction, just curiosity perhaps, makes me think I may find some kind of new understanding at least in talking with people involved in the current war, people who now know something of the combat I was once involved in at the platoon, company, and battalion level. The idea leads me to a third location, this one on the main post area of Fort Benning, completely at the center of things. The huge, forbidding structure is called Infantry Hall but is known around the fort and among townspeople as Building Four. Building Four is the home of the Infantry School. As institutional architecture goes, even for a connoisseur of twentieth-century horrors it is the quintessential atrocity, the kind of dispiriting monolith that would be despised at a big engineering university. A huge, yellow, brick box covering acres, it is easily the size of eight or ten Wal-Marts, just baking there in the summer Georgia sun. At the main entrance, the moment is briefly redeemed by the famous "Follow Me!" statue of the infantryman.

When you get inside, oddly you stop noticing anything about the building at all. Although the bleakness continues – endless dark terrazzo floors, concrete block walls, banks of metal windows that don't open, steel doors leading to classrooms, labyrinthine hallways leading into warrens of offices and rooms cluttered with partitions and cubicles – you just don't see it. Instead, you see the people. Moving about, talking, almost electric with energy, there are young officers and NCOs all over the place. One sees no formal uniforms of the sort we used to call class A. People are dressed in a variety of combat fatigues: some wear the dark jungle uniform, many the desert version, others the new, general-purpose, multiservice design you see on army, air force, and marine personnel. Individual uniforms are distinguished by the heraldry of the wearer's particular experience and calling. On tabs near the breastbone they display insignia of rank. On their left shoulders they wear the identification of their current units. On their right shoulders they wear their combat patches – a riot of famous line-unit insignia – the First, Third, Fourth, Ninth, Twenty-fourth, Twenty-fifth Infantry Divisions. The Tenth Mountain. The 82nd and 101st Airborne. The First and Second Armored. Some have served with the Rangers. Others have come from the Special Forces. The company-level officers and NCOs are in their twenties and thirties; the instructors and the military faculty in their thirties and forties. They come in all shapes and sizes, although most of them are obviously physically fit. They are men and women; white, black, Hispanic.

At the reception desk, a couple of young OCS cadets spring to their feet to help me with directions. An NCO at the desk takes over with that kind of "God these young officer types get stupider every year" voice I remember so well and tells me what I want to know, which is how to find some instructors in tactics, operations, current command and control doctrine, and the like. On my way to the elevators I talk to several young captains, with combat patches from a variety of major units, who say they are in the career course. They are smart, polite, humorous in a young-officer kind of way, but also thoughtful and quite articulate. They talk with pride about their units and the commanders they have worked with.

In the elevator, I ask a major riding with me to confirm the directions I've been given. He does and says that in fact he's going there right now. Come along, he says. He looks to me like your basic young infantry major. He turns out to be a chaplain. I realize that I cannot recall ever talking to an army chaplain before. I always shied away from them in Vietnam—they gave me the willies, as did the idea of their praying over me. This guy, on the other hand, is pure Nashville. His name is Acuff. I want to ask him if he is one of the musician Acuffs, but I forget. When he finds out I'm an English professor from Tuscaloosa, he tells me he went to school in Birmingham. We know a number of the same people at Samford, a good Baptist university where he got his bachelor's degree before getting a master's degree in philosophy from George Mason University in Virginia. He tells me about the difference between his college English stint in the early 1970s, where they did a lot of close reading (what they called then the new criticism), and the master's program, which had gone completely over to postmodernism, the poststructuralist poetics and politics of the text. He shows me the Foucault paperback he has been reading. He is interested to hear that the pendulum seems to be swinging back, that what is called pomo (postmodernism) has now given way to what is called po-pomo (post-postmodernism). We agree that it's a jargon shift even the army would be proud of.

Pointing to his bare right shoulder, the chaplain tells me he's one of the few officers on the cadre who hasn't been to Afghanistan or Iraq. Ironically, he is now on his way to Korea. He has his son with him. He's a really nice kid. When we're talking about my service with the armored cavalry in Vietnam, he wants to know whether we had Bradleys. I have to explain to him that in those days we had ACAVs and Sheridans, which were experimental tanks, now obsolete. He wants to know if we ever had to engage Communist tanks, as our troops did in the Persian Gulf War. No, I say, what we had to look out for were mainly mines, booby traps, ambushes, and RPGs, as they do in Iraq right now.

The chaplain says he knows exactly whom I should talk to: a lieutenant colonel who currently oversees the curriculum and instruction for the infantry officers' basic and career courses, and also some transition seminars for majors and lieutenant colonels about to assume battalion command. The colonel has commanded a battalion of the Twenty-second Infantry Regiment of the Fourth Infantry Division in Iraq, the chaplain tells me. His unit went in as part of the big-unit war and then took up security operations in Tikrit, where they participated in the capture of Saddam Hussein. When I get to the colonel's office, he has just finished a conversation with a Royal Scots major, on exchange from the British army. The lieutenant colonel says he will be glad to talk with me, and asks if he can buy me a cup of coffee in the snack bar.

The officer's name is Steve Russell. We get our coffee, and our conversation lasts an hour and a half. He is everything one might imagine in a young officer. In his late thirties or early forties, he has a young, alert face and a lean, trim, athletic build, a runner's frame. He is friendly in the way that makes somebody comfortable to be around him immediately. His hair is cropped but cut like mine, civilian style, combed with a part. No white sidewalls, high and tight. It does have one distinctive feature. Unlike mine, it is completely gray.

We talk and talk, covering miles and years and generations, comparing combat memories, the kinds of troops we worked with, the kinds of command problems we had to solve. Steve tells me how things in Iraq went overnight from about the big-unit phase of the war, which took about three days, to a security mission; and how eventually it became a lot like my war in Vietnam—a war of the observation post and listening post, of the patrol, sweep, cordon, raid, and ambush, of the daytime search and clear and the night defensive position. He praises his soldiers and tells me that it bothers him deeply that nobody at home save for their friends and families cares much what they are doing, that nobody in the country has any understanding of sacrifice. But he also tells me not to feel sorry for them. They may be the kinds of young people who couldn't find jobs or wanted money for an education, but he reminds me that these enlistees are now nearly all post–September 2001. They have a distinct attitude, he says—and this is the exact word he uses—of "selflessness."

We talk about the politics of the war. I tell Steve that while I agreed with the October 2001 invasion of Afghanistan, the search for bin Laden, and the takedown of the Taliban, I oppose completely the Iraq mission as a replay of the Gulf of Tonkin scam, and think that the Washington REMFs (rear-echelon motherfuckers, we called them in Vietnam) were hell-bent on the invasion from the start, either cooking the intelligence or misrepresenting it so as to rush the country into war. I spill out my sense of helpless fury at nearly everything that has happened since, marking it all as prima facie evidence that we just keep making the same mistakes over and over again. I move on to my concurrent rage at people who don't give a shit about the war as long as it's not their kid or the price of gas doesn't spike too badly or they don't see too many disturbing things on the evening news while they try to eat supper. Most days when I read the casualty lists, I see my war: a lot of American kids dying out on the ass end of nowhere for next to nothing. They try to observe rules of engagement that often wind up getting them wounded or killed. Meanwhile, we continue killing the hell out of Iraqis in ways that the expression "collateral damage" just does not cover. In fact, I tell him I have written two very angry essays about many of these things, one about an accident of war that has killed an American on the same day the president of the United States has been prancing around in a flight suit on the deck of an aircraft carrier, and the other about the White House and Pentagon fire-eaters.

Steve says he can relate to the first essay. He is amused by the conceit of the second but tells me he has worked with a lot of the Washington REMFs I have caricatured. He says that some may be in fact pretty much the people I think they are, but that some of the others are far more complicated and thoughtful than I make them out to be. As to his own participation in a political war, he refers me to Ulysses S. Grant's *Memoirs*. He reminds me that Grant thought the Mexican War was dead wrong from the start and said so. An imperial land grab if there ever was one, Grant said, it ranked right up there with the Southern war of secession in its utter moral misguidedness. But as a serving officer, he knew his professional obligations under a constitutional system of civilian authority. Once the leadership of the country is committed to a war, the soldier's job is to get on with it and get it done. The colonel makes it clear to me that it's the only view for a professional soldier to take and stay anywhere close to sane. Any attempt to get personal political doubt tied up in professional duty usually just prolongs the killing. Unless there is an egregious abuse of lawful, constitutional authority, the military commander's job is to accomplish a mission and bring the war to an end. The oath he has taken as an officer, he reminds me, is not to the president or the Congress or any other person or body, king, dictator, presidium, or revolutionary council. The oath is to the Constitution, to a form of government, separation of powers, checks and balances, and to a body politic, ultimate military power by law conferred upon and resting in the hands of elected officials. And the commanders all know that. Further, we are far from talking about any kind of "good soldier" or "I was only taking orders" defense here. Every single one of these people can tell the difference between a lawful and an unlawful order. And they all know what a soldier is supposed to do in the event of such a difference. The oath the soldier has taken is to uphold the U.S. Constitution. If there has been constitutional abuse of power, there are clear legal and constitutional means of remedying such abuse.

As Steve talks about the nuts and bolts of the mission, the responsibilities of command and control, tactics, readiness, I arrive at a stunning realization that the war he's talking about is pretty much like mine—substitute jungle for streets, alleys, walls, ruined buildings, a war of the patrol, the sweep, the cordon, the observation and listening post, the night defensive position, the ambush. A war run by squad leaders, platoon leaders, and company commanders. I say as much, and Steve says I'm correct in this.

We talk about Vietnam. He says we lost it in 1956, when we refused to abide by our commitment to free elections, which was part of our sponsorship of the 1954 Geneva peace agreement. We lined up, he said, with a government and a leadership that simply did not represent an alternative to Ho Chi Minh and the communists comparably grounded in the will of the people. Ngo Dinh Diem was the wrong figure to back as the head of an ostensibly democratic state in every way: a Roman Catholic, a northerner, an austere dictatorial personality too deeply connected with colonialism and domination by the West. In Iraq, he says, we are finding our way toward committed, representative figures. Still, as in our football games, we want the forty-yard-long bomb and the sixty-yard run after the catch. The professional job on the ground, Steve says, is more like three yards here, a yard there, on a given day maybe five or ten more. We have succeeded in achieving a conventional military victory, hunting down Saddam Hussein, getting a provisional government, then elections, then a coalition government, then a complete cabinet, then killing Abu Musab al-Zarqawi, then telling the Iraqis that the clock is running on their security forces, their plan for establishing independent political order in the country. Whether I agree or not, I must say that for once I think I'm getting some purchase on the idea of progress—as opposed to the Washington bullshit about "staying the course," "refusing to cut and run," "not dishonoring those who have already fallen."

We talk about General Bond and whether or not he should have been on the ground with us. I understand, I tell Steve, how brigade and battalion officers commanding from helicopters in Vietnam really wanted to be with us on the ground, and how most of them were brave, conscientious officers—the frustrated middle management of combat, so to speak—trapped in a bad situation. He says things haven't changed all that much for a battalion commander riding in a Bradley or a Humvee; that one of the hardest things not to do is rush to the site of the action and start kicking doors down; that one of the hardest things *to do* in some kind of correct balance is to let subordinate commanders command without second-guessing them in combat, in the hope that they will make their own right choices while learning to develop and grow in confidence.

We talk about the marines in Haditha, all the talk—mere rumors at that time—of a massacre, another My Lai. We sort through the rumors swirling around, the news reports, the conflicting military versions. We agree how noncombatants will never understand the anger, fatigue, and frustration, fragility of emotions, that in a given unit can lead to the breakdown of leadership or discipline that takes it over the edge; we also speculate that when it happens, one can nearly always go back and see how it has been preparing itself before the event, somewhere in the particular unit nervous system. We talk about the scoop incentives of investigative journalism, and run that against what is going through the minds of officers who engage or acquiesce in false reporting, worried about their efficiency reports, unit morale, damage to the war effort or public opinion; who decide that dealing with the incident through unit channels is the least damaging response to the mission. We speculate on who will eventually be charged, tried, convicted. The patrol in question was commanded by a staff sergeant. A captain has been relieved. Will there be battalion-, brigade-, and division-level indictments? We affirm our deeply shared belief that incidents like this are totally aberrant among the myriad operations being conducted, with units going out every day and every night; that the army and the marines, especially today, adhere to a high standard of conduct.

On the other hand, sometimes something just snaps. "I don't know," Steve says finally. "We all know that he's right over there in town at V. V. Vick." We fall silent and look at each other. It is one of those spontaneous, stunning moments. Across a couple of generations and the experience of six or seven new wars between us, we both know who "he" is.

We end the conversation with Steve's remembrances of the soldiers under his command. He talks about his confidence in his captains and lieutenants, in his NCOs and enlisted soldiers. This is the best army we have ever put in the field. Eventually, we will need not only to memorialize them but also to honor them. By this he means hear their stories. The latter has become something of a preoccupation with him, he says—to the point he is going to try to do something about it—and that something is what someone like me might least expect from an officer with a career of this distinction and a future this bright in the army. If the war on terror goes on, as it surely will, somewhere he will get a brigade. The next time around it will be a division or a corps. That's how impressive this guy is. He is incredibly smart; logical; possessed of intellectual discernment; articulate and unapologetic for his complex ethical positions on military responsibility and discipline, duty to the country; impressively well read in history, literature, and politics.

Steve Russell is everything an old soldier might imagine today's young professional officer to be—and more. He's also made all the right stops on the way up. In five years he has done Kosovo, Afghanistan, and

Iraq. He's been a general's aide, a hotshot staff planner, and a successful commander of a battalion in combat. He is what we would have called in Vietnam a water-walker.

As it happens, he is getting out. Steve is only forty-three, he says. In his master's work at the U.S. Army War College he found a passion for history, and he is going to try a career as a writer. He's made some of that history, after all. He has a book planned. "A Tale of Three Cities," he may call it: Kosovo, Kabul, and Tikrit.

I am stunned. He is everything that is right and always has been right about the American professional officer corps. He is a soldier who understands that service is inseparable from ethical citizenship. I pull out of my pocket a note I had written to myself at a filling station early that morning outside Montgomery. As I made the three-hour drive from my home to Columbus, I had been thinking over my coffee, while it was getting light, about General Bond, and all the things he did in his life that led him to that dusty road outside Tan Linh, Binh Thuy Province, Third Corps Tactical Zone, Vietnam; and about Calley, and all the dreadful vectors of history that culminated in that one young lieutenant's sad, misbegotten soul during four hours in My Lai. The note reads, "what happens when our lives put us at a certain place at a certain time and force us to make choices about being actors in history?" Now, sitting in the snack bar in Building Four with Steve, I read the note aloud.

There is another long silence. We look each other in the eye for a long time. He nods in a kind of agreement, with a final look that says, "if you ever find an answer, let me know." Our conversation winds down. We promise to exchange things we have been writing. I drive home.

The next day we swap e-mails. I send an account of a talk I gave some time back to newly commissioned officers at my university. Steve sends me letters he has written while commanding the battalion in Tikrit. On the question I have read from my slip of paper, neither of us has thrown the brilliant forty-yard pass, followed by the sixty-yard touch-down run. As an old lieutenant who had the blessed fortune to survive a war and become a teacher and a writer, I feel affirmed. The mystery I have been chasing through the past has come around to meet me in the present, in the person of this officer a generation and several wars down the line from me who has dedicated himself to passing on his hard-won knowledge of leadership and ethical example to the officers of the future. I have found a companion on the long march called history at Building Four, the National Infantry School, where the question we share, in the character curriculum, remains item number one.

Steve is not the guy in the infantry statue. Nobody is. But he embodies the famous words at the base, "Follow me." What he teaches is the hardest job in the army. It is called carrying a rifle and leading. It involves passing on hard-won knowledge and ethical truths, the ones that determine whether history records a soldier as a William R. Bond or a William L. Calley.

Hajis

Hajis. This is the name our young military people use for the current enemy. Technically, a Haji is one who makes the Hajj: the pilgrimage, the journey to Mecca that Islam says every Muslim should make at least once in the course of a life. Before Haji, the slang military term of choice seems to have been Raghead. Before that, it was Camel Jockey or Sand Nigger. Whatever bad-guy word our newest generation of warriors uses, for someone of my generation who grew up on Krauts and Japs and honed his own military skills on Dinks, Gooks, Slants, Slopes, and Zipperheads, it's a long way from Tin Pan Alley's "The Sheik of Araby."

That 1920s song was still around during my post–World War II childhood – and I remember it from the lewd parody we sang at fraternity parties in the early 1960s. I grew up on the standard *Arabian Nights* stories about Aladdin and Ali Baba and the Forty Thieves – carefully sanitized by the removal of references to Scheherazade, the storytelling sex slave. I heard older people talk about Rudolph Valentino in *The Sheik* and Douglas Fairbanks in *The Thief of Baghdad.* I recall sports announcers calling Babe Ruth the Sultan of Swat.

The first thing I remember in any detail about Arabs or Islam was the cover of an early 1940s recording my parents had of *The Desert Song* – an album with individual sleeves for a pile of thick, brittle, old 78 rpm disks. On the front was a Sahara scene, all burnt-brown and sand-colored. The original plot involved a young Frenchman, the son of the general in charge of French colonial forces in Morocco, who affects to be an indolent, pleasure-loving ne'er-do-well. Secretly, however, assuming the guise of the Red Shadow, he is a partisan of the Arab struggle for independence, leading a band of romantic Riff bandits. Revealed eventually to be the masked champion, he is reconciled to his father and, having survived the wiles of a native dancing girl, wins the heart of the heroine who has heretofore found him contemptible. Our musical had a wartime update. Taking a cue from *Casablanca,* French colonial oppression was rewritten into Vichy villainy, compounded by collaboration with would-be Nazi enslavers of the desert peoples.

I find this jumbled up in my memory with a lot of post–World War II clutter. There was stuff my uncle brought home from service in North Africa, camel-skin wallets, strange occupation currency, a guidebook issued to U.S. troops describing Arab food, clothing, customs, social taboos. I remember being entranced by my brother's long-playing record – a hi-fi album it was called in those days before stereo – of a newer Broadway musical, *Kismet,* which somehow filtered Borodin through Rimsky-Korsakov into a bunch of people gloriously wooing each other in turbans and harem pants. On the shelf in the family room was a deluxe, Literary Guild edition of *Seven Pillars of Wisdom* by T. E. Lawrence, whom I somehow understood to be one and the same with Lawrence of Arabia. A Book-of-the-Month-Club selection I remember reading avidly was Leon Uris's *Exodus*, in which Arab foes of the brave Israelis proved luridly depraved, bloodthirsty, and vicious.

Like many Americans of my era, I also got a good bit of my cultural education at the Saturday afternoon movies. There Islam got the occasional romantic nod. One of the first films I ever remember seeing was *The Saracen Blade*, with Ricardo Montalban, suggesting that back during the Crusades, Saladin may have been a worthy warrior-king. Others of the genre included a remake of *The Desert Song*, with Gordon MacRae and Kathryn Grayson, and *The Adventures of Haji Baba*, with John Derek as a dashing young desert sheik. Modern Arabs seemed morally ambiguous at best in the movie version of *Exodus*, where the childhood best friend of Paul Newman, playing the brave Israeli Ari Ben Canaan, may have been Palestinian; but if he was, so were the slimy sadistic bastards who raped and mutilated the flaxen-haired Jill Haworth—all to the soaring strains of Arthur Ferrante and Louis Teicher. A parallel message seemed to emanate from *El Cid*, where Charlton Heston's villainous opposite number, the masked fiend Almoravides, keeps showing up with a satanic howl to announce major scenes of mayhem and slaughter. The film as a total package—called by one reviewer the best Christian movie ever made without Jesus—was alleged to carry a message of religious toleration. Meanwhile, the political plot of the hero and *his* Moorish allies triumphing over the desert barbarians told the standard story: our Ragheads versus their Ragheads.

The same was true of Hollywood epics such as *Lawrence of Arabia* and *The Wind and the Lion*. Good-guy Arabs looked like Alec Guinness, Anthony Quinn, Sean Connery; or, in a pinch, Omar Sharif. Bad-guy Arabs were murderers, rapists, and torturers, screaming crazies armed with bloodlust and fanaticism.

In American film, Arabic women appeared as exotic concubines and forbidden sex-goddesses. Transplanted by Hollywood to ancient Egypt, like predecessors ranging from Theda Bara to Anne Baxter, the definitive temptress of the sands was Elizabeth Taylor's Cleopatra. Domesticated and sanitized for sitcom TV, Barbara Eden combined American perkiness and tumbling blonde tresses with that wonderful harem costume, a teenage boy's wet dream: the gauzy bra, the hip-hugging harem pants, the astonishing midriff. The title of the 1965–70 show was *I Dream of Jeannie.* "Genie" and "Jeannie." Get it? Scheherazade meets Stephen Foster. You couldn't get much more American than that. Another stretch came with Rogers and Hammerstein: I got *Kismet,* but what was an Arab named Ali Hakim, played by Eddie Albert (Eddie Albert?), doing in the movie *Oklahoma!*? It took me years to see that they had substituted him for a Jewish peddler, which in a homespun epic of frontier inclusiveness might have been deemed a disturbing stereotype.

In the realm of what we used to call "current events," Arabs and other Islamic peoples got some really strange deals. A big newsmagazine feature I remember vividly from the early 1950s involved publicity about King Farouk of Egypt. I recall in particular a swimming-pool photograph with nubile, bikinied women in the background. The king is a mound of brown, jiggling fat, wearing sunglasses and a fez, looking in my mind's eye like some kind of big, dissolute, Coppertoned Shriner. When he was overthrown by a military dictator named Muhammad Naguib (who was in turn shortly overthrown by another general named Nasser), nobody wept.

As entertaining and even less Islamic was the great playboy-sheik of the era, Aly Khan, heir apparent to the position of "world leader" – as was the phrasing of the time – "of the Ismaili Moslems" until bypassed in favor of his son. Aly Khan, at the height of his career ambassador from Pakistan to the United Nations, in fact never really looked much like anything other than an Italian gigolo. Anyone who drove Ferraris, wore beautiful suits, and was suave enough to get Rita Hayworth to marry him and have beautiful children with him seemed to have gotten his Islam into proper cosmopolitan perspective.

Most glamorous, however, decked out in imperial splendors and fervently pro-Western, was the Shah of Iran, after his 1953 American-assisted overthrow of an intransigent nationalist reformer, the definitive version of our kind of guy in the Middle East. Like the Egyptian generals, he looked so terrific in his Western-style military turnouts, alternating with impeccable Saville Row suits, that Americans wouldn't get the vaguest idea that Iran had anything to do with Islam. The shah was the inheritor of the legendary Peacock Throne, some latter-day Darius or Xerxes attended by a parade of movie-star beautiful queens. Iran was Persia—not really Middle Eastern or Muslim at all, but more like the Caucasus, the Crimea, the steppes of Central Asia—themselves, we would learn decades later, Islamic to the cultural core. For the moment, one could add to the luster of the image of the new Iran the fact that, like our new friends the Westernizing Turks—a Middle Eastern power improbably installed as a showpiece member of the North Atlantic Treaty Organization—such a model regime offered a bulwark against Russian expansion in the area. And one could add to that, of course, vast amounts of oil.

We still had air bases in Libya. Other North African allies were widely publicized as being governed by progressive, enlightened (read pro-Western and friendly but harmless) heads of state such as Tunisia's Habib Bourguiba or the Moroccan King Hassan. An Islamic uprising got ugly in Algeria from the late 1950s well into the mid-1960s, but it was couched mainly as just another a quasinationalist "third-world" revolt against French colonialism, a North African version of the Vietnam nightmare they had handed off to the Americans. Lebanon was one place where Eisenhower sent the marines in 1958—a prophecy of bloody, anarchic, murderous Beirut in the 1970s and 1980s but at the time merely a bad dream waiting to happen. The bona fide desert monarchs, like the Turks and the Iranians, seemed definitely to be on our side. They could call themselves whatever they wanted—sheiks, sultans, kings, princes—as long as the oil kept coming in our direction. With their flowing gowns, immaculate headdresses, impeccable manners, cleanliness, and fine grooming, they were Hollywood models of proper international relationship.

Meanwhile, by the early 1960s the African American struggle for civil rights had produced a strange new variety of homegrown Islam in the Black Muslims—beneath its bizarre politics and racial metaphysics a compelling syncretism of Koranic faith and discipline with pride in African American cultural heritage. A key counterculture text emerged in the *Autobiography of Malcolm X,* centered on the titular hero's own actual experience of the Hajj, the great pilgrimage itself as the conversion experience whereby he comes to realize Islam as a faith of all peoples of all colors, cultures, and nationalities. Another postcolonial favorite, arising from the author's experience of revolutionary struggle in Algeria, was Frantz Fanon's *The Wretched of the Earth.* These were mixed in with more general 1960s non-Western cultural syncretisms and affirmations of solidarity with those whom Jack Kerouac's Sal Paradise praises—on a road trip to Mexico—as "the great fellahin peoples of the earth." Sufi mysticism was rediscovered to go along with the Tao, the I Ching, and selected texts of Hinduism and Buddhism. Kahlil Gibran, a Lebanese Christian mystic of the 1920s, was enshrined in the 1960s as the author of *The Prophet,* a quasispiritual meditation on love comprised in equal part of Omar Khayyám and the Song of Songs. On TV, Johnny Carson, in his enormous, bejeweled, stage-prop turban regularly channeled Karnak the Magnificent. A favorite novelty song of the era was Ray Stevens's "Ahab the Arab" (pronounced *AY-rab*).

As to hard geopolitics, the key piece to the puzzle of the post–World War II Middle East for any serious observer was Israel. From the late 1940s onward, whatever happened in the region, or whatever happened in the larger world as a consequence of cultural conflicts within the region, happened because Israel was there. Israel: a new nation-state consecrated as the Jewish homeland. The long historical and political claims of neighboring peoples notwithstanding, Israel was a nonnegotiable commitment of the post–World War II international community: victors and vanquished; democratic and totalitarian; capitalist, communist, and nonaligned alike. It was the first great project of the fledgling United Nations. Most important, it was a pivotal American commitment. For Americans, the Middle East meant Israel. Whatever the latest configurings or alignments of life in the region, Arab identity automatically became the dependent variable, the Y term, in a complex geopolitical equation in which X, the independent value, always marked the spot, and X was always Israel.

With the United States as the standard-bearer of the West and the leading Cold War power, Middle Eastern politicians generally adopted a Westernizing public-relations model of leadership from the 1950s on. Images of "progressive" North Africans and Middle Easterners were purveyed through positive publicity devoted to cultural representatives recognizable through their Western-style dress, friendliness, and – of course – easy fluency in grammatical English. In post-Farouk Egypt, the fact that Nasser was a military dictator was conveniently forgotten. As long as he wore his British khakis and spoke with a proper accent he seemed a worthy representative of the land of the pharaohs. The West deemed him a progressive, new-model Arab leader until he and his Syrian counterpart, remodeling their countries into the short-lived United Arab Republic, suddenly took up with the Soviet bloc – at which juncture it seemed only right to most Americans that they and the Jordanians, who briefly yoked themselves to the Syrians in the Arab League, would *all* get their asses kicked in the 1967 Six-Day War between the Arabs and Israelis. And then, in 1973, with the Egyptians under a new military regime led by Anwar Sadat and the Syrians under a fledgling dictator named Hafiz al-Assad, they would try it again. As with the first war, they were defeated by mediagenic Israeli leaders allegedly employing audacious, Western-style tactics carried out by well-disciplined elite formations. The military hero of the first war, complete with pirate's swagger and matching eye patch, was the rakish Moshe Dayan. That role in the second would be filled by a hard-charging tank general named Ariel Sharon. The Arab armies, in a TV prefiguration of America's desert wars, were depicted as hapless cannon-fodder shredded and burned alive with their Communist-bloc hardware. Only incidentally Islamic, perhaps, and rallying under the banner of united Arabs, they were the uniformed myrmidons of Mideastern nation-states up against internationalist promotion of the new Israeli nationalist presence in the region.

After the 1973 debacle, Arab regimes such as Syria, Egypt, and Iraq would fall under Middle Eastern versions of basic twentieth-century dictatorships, with figures such as Assad in his dark suits, Sadat switching between elegant uniforms and mufti, and Saddam Hussein in his Baath Party fatigues and beret. To a man they looked not all that unlike their central European and Latin American counterparts. Jordan's dashing King Hussein, in contrast, would increasingly become the Western model of the enlightened Arab, complete with a honey-haired, Princeton-educated American wife, an airline heiress of impeccable Arab American descent. In politics and dress he would thereafter shift carefully among required images, alternating British-style military tailoring with business suits and traditional robes and Arab headdress. The chief international power figure in the region would remain an Egyptian, Anwar Sadat. He, in contrast to his fellow military dictators, would style himself in the Hussein-style Westernizing mold, eventually signing, during the American presidency of Jimmy Carter, the 1978 Camp David Peace Agreement with Israeli President Menachem Begin—in the latter case, with convenient American amnesia of Begin's role as a major National Military Organization terrorist against the Arabs and British during the formative era of his nation. For his efforts, Sadat would be bloodily assassinated three years later by fundamentalist Islamic radicals. He would be replaced by Hosni Mubarak, yet another general styling himself as Arab politician in the mold of the business-suited international player, making the occasional accommodation at home or abroad, but firmly presiding over a standard Mideastern military autocracy that has now lasted for more than two decades.

Along with such particular developments, the larger picture of trouble in the Middle East was getting very complicated, with new images and ideas of bad-guy Arabs popping up everywhere—including a lot of places Americans had previously tried rather carefully not to look in. Palestinians in Israeli-occupied territories undertook intifadas, the holy campaigns of military and terrorist operations against Israel and those around the world deemed friendly to Israelis. The Israelis, in turn, began to mount what became decades-long campaigns of military and undercover terrorist responses, including shellings, air strikes, raids, occupations, and targeted killings of opposition figures.

Outside the region all hell started to break loose as well. Overnight, the print and electronic media filled with so many Middle Eastern crazies that no one could keep track of them. A shadowy group calling itself the Palestine Liberation Organization (PLO), ostensibly under control from 1969 onward of a rising international figure, Yasir Arafat, undertook hijackings of commercial airliners in skies around the globe, including one spectacular early 1970 feat in which four planes were intercepted en route to New York City. In 1972, a PLO faction made history as terrorist hostage-takers at the Munich Olympic Games. In a bloody rescue operation by the German authorities, Israeli athletes were shot down along with their suicidal captors. In another such crisis with a happier ending, after the 1976 diversion of an Israeli flight to Entebbe, Uganda, the world would learn of a miracle rescue by an elite force of Israeli commandos in which all the terrorists would be killed during the safe rescue of all hostages (the only Israeli casualty would be a young colonel named David Netanyahu, the brother of future Prime Minister Benjamin Netanyahu, killed while commanding the rescue force). Such good news would become a rarity. The norm, rather, would be hostage dramas enacted on one tarmac after another, or in one notable case, multiple commercial airliners parked in the desert exploding one after another. El Al Airlines passengers were machine-gunned and grenaded at airport ticket counters in Rome and Vienna.

Such acts of terrorism began to take a particularly menacing turn for Americans as well. In a June 1985 incident, airliner hijackers tortured, beat, and murdered a U.S. Navy diver, Robert Stethem, shooting him execution-style in the head and dumping his body from the plane at Beirut International Airport. In another later that year involving a Mediterranean cruise ship, the *Achille Lauro*, Leon Klinghoffer, an elderly American Jew, was executed and his corpse then pushed over the rail in his wheelchair. In the mid-1980s Lebanon had become the epicenter for interminable hostage dramas involving Westerners. There were murders, rescues, bizarre deals, unexpected liberations. Hostage negotiators themselves became hostages of factions and splinter factions. Violent terrorist wings sprang up under a host of names: Hamas and Black September, Hezbollah and Islamic Jihad. In Beirut alone there seemed to be so many brands of crazies that Western journalists started calling them all "looney tunes."

But this was no cartoon. Each week seemed to sprout its crop of incensed, menacing, ruthless, homicidal Middle Easterners. Americans rationalized the spreading violence as a problem specific to the Middle East: somehow Arab related, in many cases obviously Israel related, but still not really Islam related. The oil-related embargo of 1973 and formation of OPEC could be seen as almost comforting in this respect: its origins, we convinced ourselves, were really grounded in global economics. Then as now, Americans did their best to imagine all those oil ministers in the Western-style suits at the latest OPEC meetings, sitting with the odd sheikh in flowing robe and headdress. Keep thinking about it long enough and the men in Western dress start to look Venezuelan. Or, if a problem could be identified with what seemed an increasing Islamic militancy, one could still note a host of almost surreal cultural divisions among Muslims themselves.

For a while comic relief was provided by Libya's braying pan-Arab Mu'ammar Gadhafi, the West's favorite Islamic wild man, fanatic, idiot, clown, megalomaniac. Every so often we got to shoot down a couple of his air force jets over the Mediterranean; later, in retribution for alleged harboring of terrorists, there was a memorable cruise-missile strike on one of his family compounds in the desert. We missed him but killed his five-year-old daughter. Other regional leaders were killed by their own people. In 1975, King Faisal of the Saudi Arabian royal family was assassinated by an extremist from his own country. In 1981, it was Sadat in Egypt. In between, Shah Mohammad Reza Pahlavi of Iran was taken down in 1979 by an Islamic revolution in which a decadent, wasteful, glittering, albeit unreservedly pro-Western kingly rule—supported by a vast secret-police apparatus of repression and terror—was replaced overnight by an austere, militant, militarily and politically aggressive theocracy, ruled over with new absolute authority by a charismatic mullah, the Ayatollah Khomeini, a national savior returned from long exile, it seemed, much like Lenin to Russia in 1917 or Ho Chi Minh to Vietnam in 1945. Amid the upheaval, a radical faction stormed the American embassy in Iran in 1979. Fifty-two U.S. citizens were held hostage, mocked, and humiliated—along with the United States at large—for 444 days. An abortive special-operations rescue mission in April 1980, involving an elite helicopter strike force, self-destructed during a night sandstorm in the desert. Americans palliated their impotent rage with wordplay jokes on Islamic terminologies, such as "The Aya-tollah is an assa-holla" and "Kick the Shi_te out of Iran." The founders of the Islamic Revolution seemed to delight in ostensibly manipulating the hostage drama into a drama of American electoral politics at the highest level, which in the opinion of many at home and in Europe propelled Ronald Reagan into the U.S. presidency.

The joyous, much-heralded 1981 hostage release resulted in a massive welcome-home celebration, but for policy makers it also resulted in a new concept of the international reach of Islamic terror. Power, manifest as life-and-death authority over large numbers of Americans, had unquestionably been in the hands of the radical Islamic fundamentalists until they had deigned to release it. The power of Islamic terror, likewise, increasingly became the power to strike anywhere, anytime, including the 1983 deaths of more than two hundred U.S. servicemen by a suicide bomber at a barracks in Beirut.

Americans who so wished could still allow themselves to be briefly distracted from concern for the safety of Americans by the odd internal catastrophe in the region. Along with the hostage taking, a long, meatgrinder Iran-Iraq war also began in 1979, with two conventional armies assaulting each other on a level of carnage in its use of trench warfare, poison gas, and bloody frontal offensives not seen since World War I. The same year the Soviet Union invaded Afghanistan, banking against Islamic revolutionaries attempting to overthrow a corrupt secular dictatorship—and suddenly discovered, Americans became fond of saying, the Russian name for Vietnam. We admired Afghan freedom fighters who called themselves mujahideen. We didn't care at the time that they had religious plans for a fundamentalist Islamic state; nor did we dream they would provide the basic combat training for a cadre of Islamic internationalists including such figures as a young Saudi Arabian political and religious zealot named Osama bin Laden. Mujahideen: the name sounded good. It even sounded good in translation: holy warriors, fit for fighting a war against the Russians. The United States boycotted the 1980 Summer Olympic Games on behalf of the invaded Afghans. We relished Red Army military misadventures in the country the British called the graveyard of empires because for once it was the Russians who didn't seem to be learning from history. The Afghanistan quagmire paid out for us, still in our Cold War mentality, in what the Soviet people came to call the legend of the Zinky Boys—named for the metal in cheap

Soviet military coffins. They counted thirteen thousand dead, as many as fifty or sixty thousand badly wounded—a generation scarred by service, butchery, atrocity, and defeat.

Americans tried to extract colorful news from the mess and inject it into our popular culture. Dan Rather of CBS went on assignment in the war zone, appearing in Mujahad dress and quickly dubbed Gunga Dan. On the big screen, *Rambo III* (1988) pitted the hero—Sylvester Stallone as a Buddhist making grotesque exception to his pacifist principles— against the Russian kidnappers of his mentor, Colonel Troutman, who was on a secret mission in the war zone. Likewise, in a James Bond installment of the era, *The Living Daylights* (1987), Afghanistan became a hot spot for heroes and villains duking it out in the latest global plot. Much in the style of *Top Gun*, a Cold War face-off set in the Persian Gulf, movie payback was waged from the air against Middle Eastern baddies in two *Iron Eagle* thrillers (1986, 1988), the first a hostage drama involving rescue of an American pilot from the clutches of a greasy tin-pot Middle Eastern dictator, and the second the execution of a special ops plan to take out a nuclear missile site in the region.

Thus the United States consoled itself at the movies while finding itself, in the actual Middle East, still mainly embattled and impotent. Under Ronald Reagan's CIA director, American operatives during the mid-1980s attempted selective support of the most promising factions of Afghan freedom fighters as anticommunist surrogates and allies, with the collaboration of Saudi and Pakistani intelligence services. A parallel effort eventuated in what came to be called the Iran-Contra Affair, based on the revelation that the U.S. government had been selling weapons to Iran for use in the war against Iraq and using the profits to fund anticommunist rebels in Central America. Meanwhile, terrorism continued to dominate the news. In 1988, a Pan American Airlines jetliner was blown out of the sky over Lockerbie, Scotland, in a plot eventually revealed to have been engineered by two Libyans. In the same year, an Iranian airliner full of civilians was shot down by a high-tech ground-to-air missile launched from a U.S. Navy guided-missile frigate in the Gulf of Basra.

Satisfaction and a much-needed clarity of purpose arrived in Operation Desert Storm, or what has now come to be known as the First

Gulf War or the Persian Gulf War, a direct response by a U.S.-led coalition to an Iraqi invasion of Kuwait. Through endless television coverage led by the then-novel, around-the-clock news channel, CNN, the nation witnessed the first war in American history ever to look completely like a video game (the thoroughness of the illusion remains, one might add, with just a handful of ground combat movies ever produced, such as the 1996 Meg Ryan–Denzel Washington vehicle *Courage under Fire* and the 1999 George Clooney gold-heist thriller *Three Kings*). That war (1990–91) spawned a host of popular journalistic, historical, and autobiographical accounts. Major military commanders, virtually all having won their leadership lessons skills the hard way as junior officers in Vietnam, became new national heroes: Colin Powell, Norman Schwarzkopf, Barry McCaffrey, and others. Political leaders such as U.S. President George H. W. Bush and Secretary of Defense Dick Cheney were credited with assembling and holding together a multinational force of thirty-four nations—"the coalition," it was called, with its heavy power derived from Western armies. But they also constantly publicized, as the nemesis of the Iraqi dictator Saddam Hussein, the coalition's co–high commander, Khalid bin Sultan (a three-star general Saudi prince) and representatives of other Arab allies including, in addition to invasion-victim Kuwait, Bahrain, Qatar, Oman, and the United Arab Emirates.

A 1993 military exercise against warlord-terrorists in Somalia ended more dismally, with nineteen U.S. soldiers killed, seventy-three wounded, and thousands of Somalis killed in the battle of Mogadishu—a tactical disaster that the 1996 film *Black Hawk Down*, to Hollywood's credit, bothered little to conceal behind its rah-rah, special-effects spectacle. That the theater of war was an Islamic locale might be inferred from the customary opening sequence, the vista of a sun-baked city accompanied by the sound of calls to prayer from minarets. A daring attempt by elite American military forces to snatch a murderous bandit chief stirs up the place like a giant anthill. The dark-skinned inhabitants rove the streets in bloodthirsty hordes, ambushing Americans on the ground with automatic weapons and shooting down their helicopters with shoulder-fired rockets, but largely exercising a military talent for being mowed down by the boatload by a bunch of MTV grunts just happy to get out alive.

A similar vision of the enemy pervades *Rules of Engagement*, a military hostage-rescue drama set in Yemen. In it, an elite force commanded by a black U.S. Marine colonel is sent to evacuate the American ambassador and his family. The mission is accomplished, but during withdrawal the colonel believes that an enormous mob menacing his force is about to pull out concealed weapons and attack them, so he preemptively calls in heavy firepower that kills countless civilians. The drama plays out as a flashback during a court-martial in which the African American colonel, about to be made a scapegoat, is defended in the courtroom by a tired, cynical white colonel who once saved the black colonel's life in Vietnam. Here the ethnic sanitization of the Islamic menace is particularly ingenious: again, depict the enemy as murderous hordes, mow them down, *and then* complicate the problem of command response under fire with so many issues of American memory—Vietnam, race, generational disillusionment, and the like—that we really don't think about all the locals getting blown up.

In parallel soft-imaging of Islam as Arabian Nights popular-culture fantasy, one of the great Hollywood box-office entertainments of the early 1990s turned out to be Walt Disney's cartoon-adventure *Aladdin* (1992), albeit in a version heavily reedited—as a gesture of post–Desert Storm magnanimity—after trial showings gave offense to Arab viewers. Menacing, hook-nosed, scimitar-twirling Arab villains became secondary players in a vehicle for Robin Williams as the voice of the genie. The young lovers Aladdin and Jasmine look and sound like American teenagers. Similar sanitizations mark the *Diehard* series of international terrorist action films featuring Bruce Willis. After taking heavy criticism for drawing the Middle Eastern villains of the first installment in luridly ethnic caricatures, later films in the series recruited their terrorist trash from Europe and other non–Middle Eastern places.

Meanwhile, life imitated art. As if the Islamic politics of Africa, the Middle East, and Central Asia were not sufficiently troubled and confusing, from 1991 onward the world witnessed successive outbreaks of genocidal ethnic and religious warfare in the Balkan states, the former Yugoslavia. Predominantly Eastern Orthodox Serbs renewed ancient religious wars against the Muslims of Bosnia-Herzegovina, with slaughters spreading among Croats, Slovenes, Montenegrins, Macedonians, and Albanians. A dread new phrase was needed to describe the terror: "ethnic cleansing." In a 1995 massacre, as many as seven thousand Bosnian Muslim males were killed by Bosnian Serbs. In 1999, Kosovo became a center of bitter fighting between Serbs and ethnic Albanians; its very name was a commemoration of the bloody conquest of the region six hundred years earlier by the Turks. Throughout the war, U.N. peacekeeping forces were deployed, including major U.S. ground and air combat formations. Meanwhile, an influx of jihadists from Africa, the Middle East, and Central Asia transformed the region into a training ground for Islamic fighters.

In the middle of these events came the New York World Trade Center bombing of 1993 in which six Americans were killed. Eventually tried and convicted of the crime were a radical sheik from Brooklyn and a ragtag bunch of conspirators. In 1996, another bomb at a U.S. military barracks, this time in Saudi Arabia, resulted in eighteen U.S. service members killed and 372 wounded. Bombs destroyed American embassies in Kenya and Tanzania in 1998. In 2000, a suicide attack heavily damaged the destroyer USS *Cole* in the Gulf of Aden. Increasingly, a single figure, Osama bin Laden—the renegade heir to a Saudi construction fortune who had learned his terrorist skills among the mujahideen during the Afghan War against the Russians—emerged as the suspected mastermind of such attacks worldwide.

The threat of global terrorist conspiracy by Islamic radicals with bin Laden at the head was catastrophically realized in the World Trade Center and Pentagon attacks of 11 September 2001, when, just after takeoff from American airports, four Islamic hijacker-pilot teams turned fuel-laden airliners filled with passengers into flying bombs. The pilots had all received flying instruction at American flight schools. The leader was an Egyptian, and the other conspirators included a preponderance of Saudis who had mainly been recruited and prepared for the mission in Europe. As their converging paths were traced, their stories as killer Hajis were those of average men willing to commit suicide with the intent of wreaking spectacular destruction and taking with them as many Americans as possible.

American military retribution was swift and precise. U.S. forces rolled into Afghanistan in October 2001, where Al Qaida had been headquartered. The Islamic government of the Taliban was rooted up and replaced, though bin Laden and his cadres continued to operate in the border regions with Pakistan. In spring 2003 came the lightning conquest of Iraq and the eventual capture and overthrow of the old villain of a decade earlier, Saddam Hussein. The problem once again, Americans were told, was not Islam but Al Qaida support and possible weapons of mass destruction.

Even as conventional military victory was being declared in May 2003, the real war began. American units bogged down in campaigns against insurgents, Iraqis joined by an inexhaustible supply of Islamic fighters drawn from around the region and the world. The commander was identified as Jordanian. The insurgency capitalized on internal divisions festering since the end of World War I, when three ethnic cultures had been jammed into a geography that looked good on some peacemaker's map—Sunni and Shiite Muslims to the south and center, Kurds to the north. The overturned dictator had been of the Baath Party, minority Sunnis who had frequently employed state terror to dominate the majority Shiites. Hussein had carried out genocidal attacks against Kurds with poison gas. But the postwar politics of slaughter turned mainly on the two old warring factions of Islam, Sunni and Shiite, locked in ancient, homicidal hatred. Meanwhile, porous borders allowed a virtually unstoppable influx of Islamic fighters from every corner of the world seeking simultaneously to kill Americans and with massive campaigns of civilian terror to destabilize any progress toward Western-style postwar government. As of this writing nearly three thousand U.S. troops have died; around 150,000 Iraqis have probably been killed, at least two-thirds in terrorist suicide bombings.

Elsewhere, in 2003, Indonesian Islamic radicals bombed tourist nightclubs in Bali. The preponderance of victims were Australian and British. In 2004, coordinated train bomb attacks killed 191 people in Madrid, Spain. The bombers were mostly Moroccans, led by a Tunisian. In the Netherlands, a son of Moroccan immigrants defiantly proclaimed both "conviction" and "hate" during his trial for the murder of a Netherlandish filmmaker, shot down in the street, his throat slashed, a note pinned to his body with a knife bearing verses from the Koran. His actions he proclaimed to be justified by "the law that instructs me to chop off the head of everyone who insults Allah or the prophet." Train and bus bombings in London killed fifty-two persons and wounded more than seven hundred in July 2005. The bombers were three British-born Islamic jihadists of Pakistani descent and one Jamaican convert. The organizer was identified as a British Muslim of Indian descent. Two weeks later, four more bombs misfired. The would-be terrorists included an Eritrean, two Somalis, and a naturalized East African. Suicide bombers at Egyptian seaside resorts two weeks later killed mostly Egyptian vacationers and workers. At first they were suspected to have been Pakistani; shortly it was realized that they, like the majority of their victims, were native Egyptians, Sinai Bedouins, increasingly displaced by the local hotel industry.

Thus continue to appear, more quickly than their places in history can be recorded, the myriad faces of Islamic terror in a Holy War that from the end of the Cold War has known no boundaries. Individual nations attend to terror according to the particularities of such bewildering global proliferations. But for the most part, at the level of governmental or managerial solutions they still try endlessly – and hopelessly – to address the issue at large by concentrating on approaches to "Middle Eastern" problems ratified by centuries of traditional geopolitics. Somehow "regional stabilization" will make things work; if all else fails, "coalition warfare" will bring about "regime change" in the name of "democracy building." In America, we sniff out trends, augur developments, try to predict or manipulate the future by the flick of a diplomatic attitude. We laud the announcement of elections in Egypt. We praise Lebanon for throwing off Syrian influence. We read a *New York Times Magazine* profile of Syrian President Bashar al-Assad suggesting that he may be something of a secret Westernizer. We declare in advance that announced elections in Iran under the mullahs will be a joke, and then we have to come up with a plan B of criticism when a relative moderate cleric is replaced as president by a radical secular conservative, an advocate of the poor and enemy of corruption intent on pursuing nuclear power status. We go back to the drawing board, at least touting progress in Afghanistan and Iraq and the steady development of democratic institutions in the Middle East.

Alternatively, we turn it into a doomsday apocalyptic fantasy wherein a uniform, monolithic conspiracy of evil is orchestrated by satanic masterminds sitting in their secret, undiscoverable nerve centers and sending out their minions in cells, not unlike those of 1950s red-scare or space-alien or atomic-mutant thrillers. Under this scenario we take them on as we have to, one by one by one; yet we can't keep ourselves from envisioning it all as some kind of monstrous postmodern Hydra. We talk endlessly about how we failed to see the whole beast through the fog. The elusive secret to the problem will be found, we believe, if we can just behead the whole poisonous monster.

The model of apocalyptic struggle, we have persuaded ourselves, is 11 September, the American apotheosis of international terrorist conspiracy. On a single morning, four U.S. airliners fly out of two different airports with a total of nineteen hijackers who have managed to penetrate American border and airport security. Flying separate courses, two of the planes take down *in sequence*—one-two, just like that—the twin towers of the World Trade Center in New York, the same World Trade Center bombed in the 1993 conspiracy by another cell. A third wreaks simultaneous destruction and death on the Pentagon in Washington DC. A fourth, diverted by passenger action, crashes in a Pennsylvania field, killing everyone aboard but no one on the ground. It is said the White House was its target, though we will likely never know for sure. Further accounts detail other would-be suicide crews scrambling off grounded planes before airport security personnel can react and detain them.

Why has the model become globalized into a myth of the doomsday imagination? The answer is simple: because it has become in our eyes so luridly media-made American. Because the signature event has happened in America, and because it has involved so many symbols of American technology, enterprise, and power, it becomes so spectacular and unimaginable that it must be the work of some unearthly evil genius. And then the evil genius vanishes into a secret hideout in the vast, faraway reaches of desert space. Somewhere up on the Afghanistan-

Pakistan border lurks Al Qaida and the shadowy bin Laden; its tentacles reach to al-Zarqawi in Iraq, and others extend to Madrid, London, Cairo. It has to be all one enterprise, we imagine, sprung whole out of the unbodied Mephistophelian air. But here exactly we forget that Al Qaida is a corporate enterprise in the fullest sense of that term; these are human agents, working together in the real world. Their motives may strike us as demonic and their crimes as fiendish, but in fact they have human minds in human bodies. Further, they are a corporate enterprise among other corporate enterprises, comprising no multinational conglomerate, but rather remaining decidedly finite, and assuming no particular order, country, or pattern. For every Al Qaida there is a Hezbollah, an Islamic Jihad, an Al Fatah, an al-Aqsa Martyrs' Brigade. Within major individual Islamic countries alone, insurgents are known to operate in Egypt, Pakistan, Algeria, Iran, Chechnya, Turkistan, Kurdistan, Dagestan, Sri Lanka, and Kashmir.

Meanwhile, back in the American dream factory, we keep making movies about old stories, turning back the clock as only we can. In the 2004 film *Hidalgo*, starring Viggo Mortensen, we devise a plot of cultural interaction between Americans and Arabs as a western translated into a Mideastern desert saga by way of *Lord of the Rings* stardom and celebrity. Mortensen, who is implausibly Nordic looking, plays a half-white, half–Native American frontier adventurer, with his horse, Hidalgo, the last of the great open-range mustangs. As an army dispatch-rider, he witnesses the 1890 massacre at Wounded Knee. He then works as an entertainer in Buffalo Bill's Wild West Show, prostituting his talents and those of his legendary horse, dissipating into drunkenness and despair. Just then, the minions of a great sheik—one an epicene, Westernized, top-hatted freak, the other a greasy, well-fed traitor (it turns out) in a burnoose with small scimitar—show up to deliver a racing challenge to be played out on the vastnesses of the Arabian desert against the monarch's prize stallion. The desert patriarch, played by Omar Sharif, is an aging ironist with a protofeminist daughter who rebels against her culture's restrictions on women; he is softened in his attitudes toward both the daughter and the infidel challenger by their brave help in unmasking the depredations of an evil nephew intent on usurping the throne. During the race the hero dispatches a bad Arab rival and wins the respect of a good Arab rival. Mortensen wins the race but does not marry the Arab princess. He goes back to America and turns Hidalgo loose. The tough little mustang, with the Spanish name meaning "noble," triumphs over the exotic, decadent, overbred Arabians. The prize is eternal freedom.

In 2006 came the direct attempt to find heroism amid desert conflict in a weekly television series, *Over There*, about a military unit fighting the current war in Iraq. Produced by Steven Bochco, the original network genius of *Hill Street Blues*, the show appeared briefly on the FX channel (FX standing, of course, for Special Effects) before being torpedoed by low ratings. As a Bochco product it was predictably graphic and full of unpleasant truths: American kids in fatigues killed Iraqi women and kids; insurgent fighters killed American kids. Plot lines were straight from the latest news: American soldiers think they have shot up civilian cars by mistake; they find dead insurgents in the trunk. Two frontline women, part of the new volunteer army, get into a fight that threatens unit integrity. A black kid questions white authority. A wise, cautious sergeant tries to keep members of the platoon alive. A fire-eating, glory-seeking lieutenant tries to get them all killed. The platoon stoner tries to stay mellow. The rest of the troops play with their cell phones, laptops, PlayStations, MP3s, still looking not all that different from what Michael Herr called in *Apocalypse Now* a bunch of rock-and-roll kids with one foot in the grave. An updated *Full Metal Jacket* or *Platoon*, the short-lived *Over There* was the latest version of cowboys and somebody-or-other, where the latter exist mainly as pop-up targets or laid-out bodies after accidents of war.

Our troops call them Hajis. We call them Arabs; Muslims; Islamic fundamentalists, Islamists, Islamofascists; terrorists; jihadists. One national news network insists on calling suicide bombers homicide bombers. They call themselves mujahideen, martyrs, holy warriors. Al Qaida means "the base." Hezbollah means "party of God." Hamas means "zeal" or "courage." Al Fatah is an acronym for Movement for the National Liberation of Palestine. Islamic jihad means what it says – even we don't have to be told that anymore.

"Even we," I say, attempting to move these thoughts, finally, from "I/me" – a former combatant from an old war abroad with bad names for the bad guys – to "we/us," a nation fighting a new war abroad against an enemy our soldiers call hajis, but also since 11 September 2001 finding ourselves in a larger war at home and around the globe where every noncombatant is a potential combatant. Yet the real problem with the enemy remains, of course, how we continue to imagine "they/them"; and, for all the appeals to a larger, plural understanding I wish some-how for us all to conceive, I must admit that my own responses are frequently not wholesome. Reading the new casualty lists and remem-bering the people in my old unit who did not come back, I want to kick ass and take names. Seeing the broadcast image of an al-Zarqawi or a video beheading, I want to exterminate the brutes, as Joseph Conrad's Kurtz says in *Heart of Darkness*. It takes everything I can do to remember a lesson from Vera Brittain's memoir of World War I British volunteer nursing duty, *Testament of Youth*. But remember it I will. In an important moment of reading and writing epiphany, she tells us that what makes it so easy for us to kill people is that we do not have the imagination to contemplate the possibilities of other peoples' thoughts, hopes, spiritual directions, inner lives.

How thus do we comprehend the Hajis? On our part, we might be-gin by sorting out our own categories of fixation with the enemy. To con-template even basic terms and categories, we might at least start reading texts like *Faith at War*, by Yaroslav Trofimov, a Ukrainian with an Italian passport fluent in Arabic, recounting his journey both geographical and ideological through what he calls "the Islamic universe": Yemen, Bosnia, Saudi Arabia, Tunisia, Lebanon, Egypt, Sudan, Afghanistan, Iraq. There, he tells us, what we see is simply not what they see. We see the war with the Hajis as a war against terrorism, whereas they see it as a war against Islam. We need to understand that the vast majority of the Muslim world believes that the current killing in Iraq is a direct result of the American invasion – a statement about the war that, whatever the official justifica-tion, begins and ends by being true. We need to realize that a Western understanding of a holy text – even a scripture – doesn't really compre-hend the Koran; that, unlike the Judeo-Christian Bible, it is not just the

Word of God but, whenever spoken or read or remembered or recited, the very person of God.

We see fundamentalist Islamists as monsters, mullahs, masterminds, mad religionists. But even when they make the newspapers we see that they are, for the most part, astonishingly ordinary looking men (our first step toward even rudimentary understanding might be to notice that, save for a miniscule number of Palestinian women, or lately, a Belgian convert, they are male). Some have beards, moustaches, Yasir Arafat/King Abdullah stubble; they generally do have brown skins, although the tones range widely; generally, they have short hair; when engaging in a mission they are usually clean-shaven and nearly always in Western dress — T-shirts, cargo pants, running shoes, backpack, resembling a cross between college students and members of a garage band. In fact, if you look at the carefully clipped stubble and desert tan, they don't look all that different from Viggo Mortensen.

Average or *ordinary* is not even the right word. The right word would be more like *nondescript.* There is, for example, Osama bin Laden: most Americans now know what he looks like. But once you get beyond that top tier, even his number-two — an Egyptian medical doctor, although in similar dress, with a similar beard, wearing glasses — is recognizable only to a handful of security professionals, who are also generally the only people who remember his name. Most of us can still name al-Zarqawi, but our picture of him is literally nondescript, in one photo a scrawny, empty-eyed, young Muslim wearing a skullcap; in another, smiling, a reasonably happy guy who has picked up some middle-age heft. Of the nineteen September 2001 hijackers, who among Americans can forget the basilisk gaze of Mohamed Atta? Yet which of us can remember a particular name or face for any of the other eighteen? We vaguely remember a name and a face, maybe Zacarias Moussaoui, the "other" hijacker, and his nutcase behavior in court. Somewhere along the line in our minds they all become the Iraq insurgents, the Madrid killers, the first group of London bombers, the second group of London bombers, the Sharm el-Sheikh bombers in Egypt.

Sometimes we get photos. Sometimes we get videotape. The faces of the dead get mixed up with the faces of the killers. We reach the point where we don't want to read their faces, nor the faces of their victims: women, children, youths, and elders—complex people with complex sensibilities and spiritualities. We have only one recourse. One way or another we just have to keep trying to get behind those faces, to look inside those heads and hearts and find out what makes them, as they say, tick. Otherwise, your average Haji probably remains for the moment exactly what we think he is. Just one more bomb waiting to go off.

What I Learned in the Green Machine

Some months back, as an English faculty member at my university for three decades and an armored cavalry platoon leader thirty-five years ago in Vietnam, I accepted an invitation from the army ROTC unit on campus to speak at an annual social event called the military ball. To anyone who has served in uniform in one of the armed forces, such festivities—formal receptions, dining-ins, unit anniversaries, and the like—are always great, high-spirited, celebratory occasions, with a long history in the military services. "Dress blues, tennis shoes, and a light coat of oil," as we used to say in the old army. I had been asked by a favorite student from one of my American literature classes, a smart, funny, hardworking guy who was about to graduate and accept his commission. As someone who had been thinking a good bit lately about old wars and young people, I readily accepted.

At the same time, in terms of personal and political attitudes, I couldn't help thinking how strangely the three-plus decades since my own army experience had brought me to the point where I could even consider accepting such an invitation. One of the last things I had done at the Oakland Army Discharge Center around dawn one day sometime in early May 1970—after having been flown into Travis Air Force Base from Bien Hoa in the middle of the night—was to take every single piece of uniform I had left, save the new class-A khakis I had been issued so as to qualify for a discount military airfare on the plane ride home, and deposit them—"shitcan" was the word we used at the time—into a fifty-gallon drum in the barracks where I had caught a few hours of sleep. Once home and back in graduate school, I grew as much unauthorized hair as quickly as possible, and, save on the rare occasion when I might run into another quiet, restless, solitary vet, tried to forget about the military and think of other things. Ditto in the mid-1970s when I began my first and last university job—the one I still cherish today—teaching and writing about early American literature on a big state flagship campus. Meanwhile, the Vietnam army experience I thought I had shitcanned began to catch up on me. Just as I found a lifelong academic subject in my investigations of life and culture in early America, so also did I find the basic myths of that culture—our incorrigible beliefs in our national exceptionalism, with their attendant assumptions of American historical innocence and geopolitical invincibility—persistently and, it seemed to me, relentlessly refigured in cultural representations of the American experience of the Vietnam War. I wrote two books about the literature of the war. Eventually I found myself able to watch some of the movies. They went into the critical mix as well. I read a lot of the history, and, with a Vietnamese friend finishing a Harvard doctorate in French, began teaching courses on historical, literary, and film representations of the war in the contexts of American, French, and Vietnamese language, life, and culture. I turned to work on a new book, *Late Thoughts on an Old War*, for the first time combining cultural reflection with autobiographical memory. Suddenly, years after I thought I had shitcanned it all, I was somehow again making my own passage through the green machine – ROTC, the officer basic course, the endless stateside training; the sudden descent into the jungle, the heat, the sweat, the sleeplessness, the black diarrhea; the boredom, the vigilance, the miserable fear punctuated by actual moments of terrified response to combat; the coming home to a place we called "back in the world," basically sentenced to silent, solitary confinement on the grounds that even if one could tell the story, there would be virtually no one in the entire country who would care to hear about it.

Suddenly, I was there again thirty-five years later, completely able to relate to them, as we used to say – the young people, the latest crop, committed to serving as platoon leaders and company commanders on the ground in a controversial, increasingly unpopular war not of their choosing. They would fight as alleged liberators in a country where they were resolutely hated – in a place, to quote Michael Herr's famous exordium from *Dispatches*, where "for years now there had been no country here but the war." Further, they would then come home to a country where, once again, the closest thing resembling any expression of public support for them, or the soldiers they would learn to live and die for, apart from the mouthings of the politicians, seemed to be "OK, OK, just as long as it's not my kid."

It was then that a more immediate problem, both rhetorical and political, hit me right between the eyes. In this case, many of the young men and women I was speaking to would be wearing their insignia of rank and branch assignment for the first time. Many of those, I realized – wearing the crossed rifles of the infantry, or the corresponding emblems of the cavalry, armor, or artillery – were already directly in the pipeline to a war that may have begun with a conventional-arms walkover but had now tactically turned into a war of the patrol, the ambush, the sniper, the booby-trap, not unlike the one I had managed to survive more than thirty-five years earlier. Further, I realized that every word I had written about the particular iron lesson of that war – learned the hardest of all possible ways by more than fifty-eight thousand dead Americans and between two and four million dead Vietnamese—that a three-thousand-year-old Asian culture really had not wanted to turn itself into a two-hundred-old Western democracy, had gone for absolutely nothing. As I watched from afar, I saw that we had furthermore compounded our history of ignorant right-mindedness with the newest version of that astounding, even catastrophic geopolitical arrogance as a millennium and a half of religious animosities fed themselves through the ethnic hatreds of twentieth-century Middle Eastern colonialism, into a world of global flashpoints where fanatical killers and suicide bombers plied the new paramilitary trade of international terrorism. Indeed, in Iraq, with our peculiar talent for historical obtuseness, we had once again pulled off, in every sense, the historically unthinkable: for however brief and bizarre a moment, we had actually gotten Sunni and Shiite Muslims to forget how much they hated each other and join in a cultural and nationalistic passion for killing Americans.

What could I say to these young people tonight—young enough to be my sons and daughters, and with even their regular-army cadre officers and NCOs young enough to have been among my first students thirty years ago? Do I say, holy shit, we're doing it all over again? Do I tell them that their commander in chief and his closest advisors got us into this on militarily and strategically false pretenses and now don't have a clue about getting us out? What good can a litany of grim historical parallels possibly do them when shortly their lives and the lives of their soldiers will be on the line? No. They had already taken the oath, I realized. They would now have to understand their duty. Officers do not get to choose their wars—although they do get to make choices, I believe now, as firmly as I did thirty-five years ago, between a legal and an illegal order. Still, this was no time to indulge in an old person's anger at the tendency of politicians to do their usual worst. Rather, it was a moment in which to appeal to a young person's eagerness to learn. Dress blues, tennis shoes, and a light coat of oil: the best way I could help these young officers was to reach far back to some leadership lessons I remembered from my old days in the army and the people I loved.

This was my new, slightly lengthened title: "What I Learned in the

Green Machine; or, the Ten Commandments, more or less, according to the worst drill cadet in the history of ROTC who somehow managed to become a reasonably competent armored cavalry officer."

And these were the lessons, I suggested, that even a butter-bar lieutenant or a university English professor might find useful in leadership and life:

1. Use your army education. Take advantage of every piece of instruction and every training opportunity you get. If you pay attention during your officers' basic course and the other professional-education opportunities you are offered from the very beginning – branch school, jump school, ranger school, jungle or desert training school – you will arrive at your first duty station as a very well trained officer – perhaps even, to your surprise, in many ways a highly qualified young person in an entry-level management position. From my own experience, after AOB (Armor Officer Basic Course) 8, Fort Knox, Kentucky, summer 1968, I found myself at Fort Meade, Maryland, with the Sixth Armored Cavalry Regiment. On the basis of my training and a lot of good help, a staff sergeant and I basically built a heavy-mortar platoon from the ground up. Thrust next into the leadership of a completely messed-up line armored cavalry platoon, with full stateside configuration of scout, infantry, and armor sections, when the former lieutenant was relieved for gross incompetence, I took them downrange the next day. Two months later, we won the squadron field training exercise. Assigned to a platoon of ACAVs upon my arrival in Vietnam and committed to the conventional work of jungle busting and ambushing, I found I was anxious – but ready.

2. Rely on your noncommissioned officers. This is so stupid even a lieutenant should remember it. All along the way, I was lucky. In armored cavalry units both stateside and in Vietnam, I found nearly always a standard complement of NCOs – an E-7 (sergeant first-class) platoon sergeant, E-6 (staff sergeant) section leaders, E-5 (sergeant) track commanders. I found out that what the books say is true: trust your NCOs, and find ways of communicating your trust while making it clear to them that you command the unit. To put it another way, let your NCOs do their jobs; don't micromanage. They really will prepare a platoon completely for an inspection, a move-out, a mission; they will also know who's in command unless you give them cause to think otherwise. Micromanaging means you don't trust them. Even worse, it means that you don't trust yourself in employing the time-honored principles of working-together, citizen-soldier, officer/NCO leadership that have made the U.S. Army the most effective army in the world.

3. *Communicate with your enlisted soldiers.* Talk with them; be available to them; and listen to them. I especially recommend the human tape-recorder principle many of us use in working with our families; let people talk, get it out in the open, while you try to repeat, summarize, identify what seem to be the important points. Again, as with your NCOs, find ways of communicating with your enlisted soldiers while making it clear to them that you command the unit. Although you probably don't need to say it, a small-unit command is not a democracy; they left the student council behind when they graduated from high school. They do not want you to be their pal or their student government representative. They want you to be their lieutenant. If and when you get a chance, seize the opportunity to do physical work with them, show that you can sweat with them, help dig holes, help break out tank rounds and load them into the turret; but don't do private-first-class work when you have platoon leader work to do. Finally, allow them their privacy; don't hang about trying to show you're a good guy when they need to be by themselves.

4. *Use the chains—I said* chains *—of command.* There are two: officers and NCOs. Young officers tend to forget the second one. In many cases where a problem might arise with enlisted soldiers, have your platoon sergeant talk to the first sergeant, and have your first sergeant talk to the battalion sergeant major. This is one of the ways, incidentally, that you can identify literature about the lives of soldiers actually written by soldiers. It nearly always talks about the twinned chains of command. In literature and life alike, you'd be amazed at how many problems manage to get solved by NCOs precisely because there's no officer trying to butt in.

5. *When you plan, make a simple plan and stick to it.* Don't outsmart

yourself and your unit. K.I.S.S.: Keep It Simple, Stupid. The world works according to Murphy's Law—if something can possibly go wrong, it will. Use simplicity in planning as a weapon against inevitable complication.

6. Use the published doctrine. It works. In a tactical situation, where quick decisions are required under tremendous pressure, let your training take over. That's why you did so much of it. In a policy situation, where some kind of administrative response is called for, consult the book. Chances are the problem is one that's already been handled a hundred times and a solution is spelled out that makes a complicated process idiot-proof. Don't reinvent the wheel.

7. Check, double-check, and, if possible, triple-check. The devil is in the details. So, frequently, is salvation.

8. Put yourself in line to do all the bad stuff first and all the good stuff last. Again, don't be a PFC when you need to be a lieutenant. But do eat last, drink last, sleep last, enjoy the benefits last, and only after you make sure the troops are taken care of.

9. When you think you can't go one step further, stay awake one minute longer, refocus even more on what you're doing, and remember: you can. You know you can. You've already done it many times before, and when people's lives are on the line, you know you can do it again.

10. As bad as it may get, remember that you are going through it with some of the best people you will ever know in your life.

On the evening I spoke to the new graduates, that last sentence brought my own experience back to me with a rush. No matter that the experience itself was thirty-five years old—nearly as old, indeed, as the regular-army lieutenant colonel sitting to my left. All of a sudden I knew exactly why I was there. This was definitely the new army—right down to the tough Hispanic kid with the Special Forces combat patch on his right shoulder, reinvesting his time as an enlisted man in an ROTC scholarship; or that semester's cadet battalion commander, sitting to my right, an Amerasian woman from an army family on Okinawa, on her way to the artillery school at Fort Riley, Kansas. Still, I knew what most of them were thinking. What will my first platoon be like? My first cadre of NCOs? My first company, or troop, or battery commander? How will we all do the first time we hit the shit? Unsentimentally, I also realized that some of them might not be alive a year or so from now. This was, after all, a university ROTC unit traditionally high in jump wings, ranger tabs, combat-branch insignia, and the like. Those that made it through, though—I knew what we already had in common. It was right there in that last sentence, the part about "some of the best people you will ever know in your life," and it was something that, as long as we lived, even time could not take away from us.

Swindled by Saint Jack

"The country made a terrible mistake last night." Thus I recall myself intoning, in some callow attempt at portentousness, to a jubilant high school classmate I still remember as the only person of my acquaintance in Adams County, Pennsylvania, to have identified himself as a supporter of John Kennedy in his 1960 presidential race against Richard Nixon. Even though we were all several years shy of the pre-Vietnam voting age—twenty-one—throughout the campaign we treated the guy as something between a weirdo and a pariah. On Election Day the rest of us were utterly shocked and astonished. Of course we all liked Ike: he and Mamie lived in Adams County. Of course we were all Eisenhower

Republicans: many of our families, English, Scotch-Irish, German, descended from the old farmer and merchant stock of the region, had been *Lincoln* Republicans. I had additional reasons. The president went to our church, where I often saw him on Sundays. I lifeguarded his grandchildren at the country club pool. On a drizzly day with no swimmers I had once even shagged golf balls for him. In the 1960 election, if Ike said Nixon was the one, Nixon was certainly the one for me.

Within two years, away at college in North Carolina, I was an unreconstructed Kennedy-ite. I would have been one whether I'd been in Michigan or New York or California. Of politics I knew little more than what I learned in high school. What I did know was that the man had some kind of style; and whatever it was, it was the kind of style that made him the kind of American man I wanted to be. From Election Day onward he had knocked everyone out with his humor, intelligence, his sheer vibrant energy and adventure with which he seemed to approach every experience. Within a week of voting day it seemed almost raffishly enjoyable that he had edged out Nixon only after his old man had gotten the Daley Machine to deliver Chicago. Ill-gotten or not, suddenly even the hairbreadth margin of victory seemed a positive thing. How long could you dwell on the threat of old-time political corruption in a person who, upon hearing a member of his administration described as "coruscatingly" intelligent, was said to have responded, "50,000 votes the other way and we'd all be coruscatingly stupid." Then came the dazzling inaugural address. Barely a paragraph in we heard him saying, "Let the word go forth from this time and place, to friend and foe alike, that the torch has been passed to a new generation of Americans— born in this century, tempered by war, disciplined by a hard and bitter peace, proud of our ancient heritage—and unwilling to witness or permit the slow undoing of those human rights to which this Nation has always been committed, and to which we are committed today at home and around the world." And then, without taking a beat, there was more: "Let every nation know, whether it wishes us well or ill, that we shall pay any price, bear any burden, meet any hardship, support any friend, oppose any foe, in order to assure the survival and the success of liberty."

At the time, it seems not to have occurred to anybody of my generation that, as was rhetorically and historically the case, Kennedy was referring, quite directly and specifically, to *his* generation – the younger, junior-officer generation of World War II, as opposed to the tired old generation of the generals such as Eisenhower – and not our own. We simply assumed he was talking about us, and so we took the challenge as our own. Then, at the end, he hammered us again: "And so, my fellow Americans," he said, "ask not what your country can do for you, but what you can do for your country." (He went on to make a similar appeal to "fellow citizens of the world," proposing that they "ask not what America will do for you, but what together we can do for the freedom of man" – a quotation that deserves at least as much to be remembered.)

Any way we looked at this, we can perhaps see now that behind the scrim of faux-Churchillian rhetoric that passed for eloquence at the time, Kennedy's speech was largely a recycling of American idealism, the standard stuff about a new vision of freedom and liberty and justice for all in post–World War II updating, in this case geopolitically mixing in Woodrow Wilson's making the world safe for democracy with domestic leftovers from Franklin Roosevelt's New Deal. But nobody had ever made any of it look or sound that way before. The youthfulness of the face, the slimness and insouciance of the carriage, the brown thatch of hair without a trace of gray, those clipped tones, the jabbing finger: "This," as the Kingston Trio hymned in a rousing, inspirational guitar-and-banjo anthem of the era, was the "New Frontier" – a musical idea those of more progressive tastes found not at all compatible with the protest songs of Joan Baez and Bob Dylan. (As the "intellectual" we reckoned Kennedy to be, he just had to be, we opined, a secret Baez and Dylan fan.) And everything truly did seem new. We were the new generation, the now generation, the generation of love, hope, and peace. We were the generation of youth. Yes, we knew that there was terrible racial hatred afoot in the country, making entire regions into landscapes of poverty, violence, and fear. Yes, we knew that the Cold War had peaked into a doomsday arms race with American and Russian opposite numbers poised to pick up the red phone and incinerate the planet in a great scenario of mutual assured destruction. Yes, we knew that our increasing commitments to an anticommunist client government in a place called Vietnam were already threatening to bring us into large-scale, direct military participation, not to mention confrontation with the Russians or the Chinese or even both. Closer to home there was the fumbling and embarrassment of the new administration's ill-conceived involvement in the Bay of Pigs debacle. On the other hand, the ensuing Cuban Missile Crisis showed that government by a new class of muscular political intellectuals—the Best and the Brightest, as they were styled—could still, if necessary, do the hard-ass, Cold War toe-to-toe with the Russians. The great line of the crisis, which an admiring press repeated interminably, came from Secretary of State Dean Rusk. "We were eyeball-to-eyeball with the other guy," he said. "And the other guy just blinked." Who could get any smarter and nervier than that?

Then, suddenly, as quickly as it had happened, it was all gone. It was early afternoon, and I was on my way to a chemistry lab. Somebody told me as I crossed a dormitory parking lot that there had been an assassination attempt in Dallas: Kennedy had been shot, but nobody knew how badly he was hurt. Like a good sophomore premed at a good college—in my own case, where Dean Rusk had paid his way waiting tables and earned a Rhodes Scholarship—I went to my lab and started the assignment. After that, my memory blurs. I must have found out sometime that afternoon that Kennedy was dead. We all glued ourselves to the fraternity-house television. I remember seeing Oswald getting shot down by Ruby, right on TV.

My most vivid memory of those days, however, is of standing on the curb along Pennsylvania Avenue that cold day in November when the funeral procession went by. A carful of us had driven through the night to get there. I don't recall whose car it was or who the other people were. I do remember that it was very cold, in the way that made even the clear, streaming, Washington DC sunlight seem almost brittle. For whatever reason, I remember what I had on: a hand-me-down tweed coat and cashmere V-neck sweater of my father's, over a button-down shirt and an English tie of the sort I had so frequently seen Kennedy wear. In some yearning way, the getup was my idea of proper New Frontier funeral attire.

In terms of total style, Kennedy was way out there: the drape of his suits, the starched immaculateness of his shirts, the simple elegance of his ties; the English shoes, the perfect haircut, the perennial tan; the aristocratic insouciance, the savoir faire beyond that of common mortals. It showed how a third-generation Irish, Boston Ward–politician Catholic could go WASP: Choate, Harvard, trust funds, society pages, and all the rest. I now seemed to understand in all the sophomoric wisdom of cultural savvy that, with Kennedy and Nixon as the presidential choices, who could have even thought of voting for the latter? Nixon's ideas were of a piece with everything outdated and, well, Republican: old-man ties, big collars, double-breasted suits, sport coats with wide lapels, fedora hats (even Eisenhower wore a homburg); imaging one of our favorite book titles of the era, he seemed the complete, harried, joyless organization man. He exuded office pallor, five-o'clock shadow, wet-combed hair; his voice was full of dreadful earnestness, droning middle-class moralism, smarmy sermonizing, *Reader's Digest* anecdotes. But it wasn't just Nixon. Alongside Kennedy, anyone else even in the rest of the Best and the Brightest—a McGeorge Bundy in his Harvard tweeds or an immaculately suited and bespectacled Robert McNamara—looked like a world-class pussy. Maxwell Taylor, the old paratroop general, still trim and energetic in mufti, looked old. Johnson, the vice president, combined drooping flesh and political commonplace with cornpone vulgarity. Kennedy exuded sex, masculinity, and power while putting it all together at some level of astonishing, unreachable elegance.

The man had more than style. He somehow embodied the moment itself of what seemed to us at the time the true possibility—not only real but reachable, the function of sinewy energy and hardheaded knowhow—of imminent national can-do apotheosis: when we nearly all believed, however briefly, that no problem existed in the world that could not be resolved stylishly, cleanly, and masterfully through American expertise, good will, material abundance, energy. Like the half-American Churchill, from whom he drew much of his rhetoric and his heroic sense of political drama, Kennedy gave us democracy with just enough royalty. He made government something out of Shakespeare or Sir Philip Sidney, with harkenings back to Machiavelli's prince and Plato's guardian of the Republic. (The mawkish Lerner and Lowe Camelot figure would come later. It says much about the era that it did not strike us at the time as even remotely sentimental.) In the closer lineage of American forebears, Kennedy took his intellectual marching orders from the polymath Jefferson, his rhetoric from the incomparable Lincoln, and his politics from the last great patrician-democrat, FDR—with the occasional nod, when quickdraw bellicosity was in order, to cousin Theodore. With leftover philosophical and rhetorical fragments of a Harvard core-curriculum erudition, and the quick bits of allusive erudition supplied by his speechwriters, John Kennedy made war and peace, peace and war, look Homeric or Augustan. He put the whole, stupid, fat, complacent 1950s on a weight-and-fitness program, turning the image of the country back out to look trim and athletic. The wartime *PT-109* legend, imaged in a popular book and custom-made tie clasps, melded the ninety-day wonder boy lieutenant with the preppie athlete, the valiant swimmer on the deserted Pacific island, surrounded by Japanese, giving it the old school try and saving his whole crew. His war pictures, with the rakish navy hat, the khakis, the dress whites, looked utterly different from those of all the old dogfaces, our fathers' and mothers' friends, now trying to squeeze into their Eisenhower jackets on Memorial Day. Of course he had been a handsome playboy after the war; but now he had found happiness as a husband and a father. He not only made uxoriousness into a virtue, he actually made *it* seem glamorous. He put the romance back into marriage, professing adoration for his beautiful, elegant, and cultured wife, suggesting that the marriage bed was that of a regal love match. He likewise rejuvenated fatherhood. Here we saw no Jim and Jane with Bud, Betty, and Kitten; no Ozzie and Harriet Nelson with David and Ricky; no Ward and June Cleaver with Wally and the Beav; no more Dick and Pat Nixon, mom in the Republican cloth coat, the kids Tricia and Julie, Checkers the Dog. His offspring somehow even rejuvenated children. These were no dour little apprentice adults. John-John and Caroline were exquisite, golden children, stylish, cosmopolitan, picture-book toddlers in the White House. In everything he said and did, Kennedy seemed to rewrite even the most exorbitant promises of democracy into a style of grace and cultivation. Huey Long said every man a king. A mawkish 1950s TV show billed itself as *Queen for a Day*. But they got it wrong. Kennedy got it right: every man is a prince and every woman a princess. That went for children, too.

The word *mediagenic* really doesn't do the Kennedy image justice. Almost overnight, a lot of us bought it completely. And it wasn't as if it didn't come with a plethora of warning labels; for many young people who caught the spell, that just sharpened the romance. With our parents' prosperous, staid Eisenhower Republicans in control of the White House and the Congress, we actively sought the restiveness of a new, edgy, vaguely proletarian intellectualism. Armed with our Sartre and Camus and homegrown testaments of rebellion such as Ralph Ellison's *Invisible Man*, J. D. Salinger's *The Catcher in the Rye*, and Jack Kerouac's *On the Road*, we took pleasure in the discomfiture of our elders who believed with all their hearts that the GOP had rescued politics from the party of immigrants, of unions, of big labor, the creeping socialism begun under Roosevelt's New Deal. Deeply connected with this in the popular mind was also Kennedy's Catholicism, which was widely discussed in the media and among voters in serious intellectual conversation. There was the fear, voiced by people of what passed for enlightened judgment, that he would in crucial instances answer not to the American people but to the pope. And behind that, there was the Irishness, the object of an anti-immigrant bias that reached back into assorted nineteenth-century bigotries and xenophobias, nativism, anti-Catholicism, even a style of cultural racism in which the Irish were frequently depicted in images resembling the negrophobic caricature of American blacks. In general politics, this lapped over into the associations of the Democratic party with the rural and blue-collar masses, of the meldings of the Jacksonian and immigrant rabbles, in the state and city machines, to combine the worst of mobocracy and political bossism. In the notorious instance of Irish Boston, John Francis Fitzgerald, Kennedy's maternal grandfather, had been the notorious rascal known as Honey Fitz, the mayor as consummate parvenu, ward-heeler, dispenser of patronage to his corrupt, grasping toadies. The other side of Kennedy's family seemed almost respectable because Kennedy could claim a grandmother who had been a domestic—a maid, and an Irish one at that. But this too for many Americans recalled an era in which a humorist like Mark Twain could always get a laugh with the line, borrowed from the newspaper advertisement page, reading "No Irish Need Apply." The best that could be said about the Fitzgeralds and the Kennedys, to use the formulas of the era, was that the breed had at least moved from shanty Irish to lace-curtain Irish. Sure, the old man had gone to Harvard and become incredibly rich, but beyond that, well, one had one's doubts.

The way Kennedy dealt with all that was masterful—and characteristic: he turned the story into a romance. If he wasn't starchy enough for the most highly placed among New England and Eastern Seaboard cultural elites with whom the clan now easily mixed, it exactly made him plenty good enough for America. The beauty of the thing was how far he and his tribe had come in a bare handful of generations. Honey Fitz turned into a charming, populist rogue, who had sired the beautiful, feisty Rose, sending her to convent school where she learned to keep the sacraments in preparation for happily mothering her brood. The old man was a harder sell: a Depression-era bootlegger, profiteer, and influence-peddler, who, having become the American ambassador to England, achieved further notoriety as an isolationist, appeaser, and perhaps even Nazi sympathizer. Now, overnight, the parvenu, the money- and power-hungry dynast was somehow transformed into the proud paterfamilias. The family's wartime tragedy now redeemed him, with emphasis on the loss of young Joe Jr., the handsome eldest son, the anointed heir, a U.S. Navy flying officer killed on a secret mission over France, and of Kathleen, the eldest daughter, the dazzling, irrepressible Kick—widowed after her British peer husband was killed in the war—dying in a postwar plane crash. The idea of dynastic duty became just the point: Jack, with his early intellectual promise, including a Harvard undergraduate thesis published as *Why England Slept*, and his own ensuing World War II PT boat heroism, was spotlighted as picking up the torch. That was the point of the whole storybook family, the wealth; the homes in Brookline, Hyannis, Palm Beach; the private schools, Harvard; new blood, so to speak, had revivified the New England tradition of enlightened political and public service, the Winthrops and the Lowells and the Peabodys, the Lodges and the Saltonstalls.

Then there was extension of the personal magic into the widely publicized new alchemy of government formation. He welcomed back the traditional Washington Democratic political and intellectual power brokers, including many of the old Roosevelt-era, Eastern-establishment ruling elites, but also reinvigorated their ranks at the top level with heavy academic infusions of Ivy League academics and innovative young policy intellectuals and management types. Particularly noted at the time was his channeling of the cerebral style of the Harvard Business School by way of the chrome and tailfin glamour of the American auto industry in the hard-nosed, number-crunching Secretary of Defense Robert McNamara. But similar cachet abounded everywhere. Secretary of State Dean Rusk was a Rhodes scholar. National Security Advisor McGeorge Bundy was the brilliant, boy-wonder dean of Harvard College. To this was added the element of roguish romance, the residue of the Irish pol legend, the personal advisors, the gatekeepers. The coinages tumbled forth from the media to describe the excitement: the Best and the Brightest, the Whiz Kids, the Kennedy Mafia. Even today such phrases are used without irony to celebrate the combination of cerebrality and ruthless expertise Americans found so exciting in so many of the Kennedy people, signature members of a dream team that he, in the image of his own scintillating personality, had managed to assemble.

Then there was the broader political wizardry of the teeming, disparate constituencies he somehow managed to assimilate and merge. One sees then and now that these were tricks no one else could likely have pulled off. The Eastern WASP establishment of law, policy, and finance people was made to get along with the unions. The populist progressives and the poor whites of the South, and the hardshell Protestant small farmers and mill workers, found common cause with the machine politicians and ward heelers, the steelworkers and coal miners, the immigrants and urban blacks, the Jews and Catholics of the North. Hollywood met Boston and New York. Chicago met New Orleans. Government became a stew of initiatives: civil rights, missile technology, counterinsurgency warfare, space exploration. Everywhere you looked there was something that looked or seemed decidedly new, usually with some snappy name testifying to its newness, some new face in a position of leadership, some new slogan pointing the way toward the future. Here was a presidency where inspiring initiatives bred themselves into a truly inspirited sense of new historical possibilities.

How Kennedy worked that out in the main, one now sees, was by a redefinition of American manhood in a way that mesmerized American men and women alike. He simply exuded what John Hellman has aptly called the erotics of a presidency. He made being an American seem sexy. Youth, athleticism, and burning, vibrant, animal energy merged with cerebrality, taste, and cool, diffident wit. Even the breathy, high-fashion Frenchness of Jackie and the stunning English beauty of the children sealed the package. Men and women succumbed completely. Especially the young.

Everywhere you looked, the world just seemed new. And young. He made our parents, his contemporaries, feel young again. Among my college cohort, he even seemed to make many of us young, after oddly growing up, as sons and daughters in the shadow of what has come to be called the Greatest Generation, in many ways so old. To seize a term that gained currency only after the 1960s, we were filled with a completely new sense of our own youthful empowerment. Whatever one tries to call the quality of spirit he seemed to us to embody so fully, it remains no-table even now, as at the time, that we didn't have the words to grasp it. We could say charm, wit, grace; but more often it was charisma, panache, esprit, joie de vivre (hubris would come later). Even when a word came along in common English, it had to be different. That is what "vigah," a great, funny word of the times, meant to us: the energy, the sinewy New England muscularity, the belief in spirited citizenship and public service – the work of an embodied idealism.

The measure of that for many of us was how suddenly, in contrast, after 22 November 1963, the world seemed old. For surely it remains one of three dates within living memory when the world changed for Americans, the others being 7 December 1941 and 11 September 2001. Quite simply, it was a day after which the world would never be the same for us. And the particular measure of that, following the assassination, was the orgy of grieving, the tidal wave of bathos and wallowing in loss in which the culture soaked itself for months and even years. A complete photographic and video record charted the terrible events in Dallas and the heartbreaking journey back to Washington aboard Air Force One. Leading the funeral procession, Jacqueline Kennedy walked in widow's garb, flanked by her dead husband's brothers, then by his brothers-in-law, then Lyndon and Lady Bird Johnson; then President Charles de Gaulle, Queen Frederika of Greece, King Baudoin of Belgium, Emperor Haile Selassie of Ethiopia; then General Maxwell Taylor, General Curtis LeMay, and the Joint Chiefs of Staff; then the Archbishop of Boston. A thousand days earlier the last would have been everybody's worst religious nightmare. Now he would outdo Billy Graham in pulpit glamour. The classic photojournalism record of it all became a monument to the great popular weekly magazines: *Time, Life, Look.* No one could be unmoved by the images: Jackie on the plane, in the blood-soaked suit, standing by Johnson as he took the oath of office; again, waiting with Bobby Kennedy on the tarmac while the casket was loaded into the navy ambulance; marching under the veil with the brothers down Pennsylvania Avenue; and then standing once more outside St. Matthew's Cathedral with the children. However ironically one looks back on it, the whole business truly was elevated to the status of classic tragedy by the immense dignity and moral heroism of his widow. A photograph of her face, with the veil lifted for a moment, during a late-night visit to the catafalque, gave the silent, impassive, grieving beauty of a medieval icon—as if a society beauty out of an Edith Wharton novel or in a John Singer Sargent painting (albeit by way of Cecil Beaton) had been invested with the repose of the queen of heaven in an altarpiece. There were the corresponding images of the children: pictures of Kennedy sailing with Caroline in his lap; the heartbreaking image of John-John giving a final salute. Along with the images came all the texts from the keepers of the word, a flood of rhetoric, much of it pseudo-Kennedy in stylistic emulation. Again the print flowed forth from the magazines and wire services. With photos it was then reissued in hardcover, limited-edition commemorative volumes with titles like *Four Days* and *The Torch Is Passed.* Here were recorded the heartbroken words, speaking the nation's heartbreak, of the old priest, the family friend, the prince of the church, a cardinal. "May the angels, dear Jack," he intoned, "see you into heaven." Here one saw the somber beauty, glamorous even in mourning, of an enormous bereaved clan kneeling before the eternal flame at Arlington. Overseas, wire services assembled photo spreads of the toothless, keening Irish balladeers, pints in hand, crying down the rain, and singing of an imagined world where John-John will be king and Caroline will be his queen. An eminent biographer, William Manchester, was commissioned official recorder of events in *The Death of a President*. Cronies weighed in with lachrymose tributes. Benjamin Bradlee of *Newsweek*, friend and fellow roisterer later of *Washington Post* Watergate fame, kept Kennedy's bad-boy secrets as assiduously as he would ferret out Nixon's political ones, effusively titling his poetic volume *That Special Grace*. "John Kennedy is dead," he concluded, "and for that we are a lesser people in a lesser land." Kenny O'Donnell and Dave Powers, two of the Irish comitatus, along with the Secret Service detail, making the world safe for the bimbo-frolics in the White House swimming pool, offered the comparably sentimental masterpiece, *Johnny, We Hardly Knew You*.

Of all such texts, only Tom Wicker's *Kennedy without Tears* remains remotely readable. And that is because, in retrospect, one sees that he captures not so much Kennedy the person or Kennedy the politician as the concept he personified to motivate a generation mesmerized by new concepts of education, enlightened citizenship, and worthy public service. Whoever Kennedy was and whatever he did or did not do, Wicker is surely right about this: JFK's importance lay in the effect of an idea he seemed to embody, the way he challenged Americans to a late-twentieth-century standard of national excellence in its classic definition. He was as close as we would ever come again to what the Greeks called arete.

For just that aspect of vigorous, enlightened citizenship I revere John Kennedy to this day, but I also resent him for it to this day. I reproach his sainted memory, sold to us along with all the rest: easy to say after the corruptions of Watergate, Iran-Contra, Monica Lewinsky, Iraq. The fact remains that a lot of us were sold on the New Frontier; sold on Vietnam; sold on civil rights; sold on America; sold on everything by a guy whose sales pitch persuaded me that here, for once, was a national figure capable of getting outside himself—as each of us could get outside our own selfish interests—and do something for other people in our country and around the world. In retrospect, that sounds like a religion; and as with all religions at one time or another, its power is now measured by loss of faith. This is to say that, like many Americans of my generation, I have now spent my later years living down my compounded reverence for and resentment of the ghost of John F. Kennedy precisely because I got to see his head blown apart by an assassin's bullet from a high-powered rifle during a motorcade in Dallas and have now lived long enough since to find out how completely fucking cynical he was about himself and the packaging job and everything else he moved Americans of my generation to do in the world. It is all damn hard to live down.

Our philosopher-king turns out to have been nothing of the kind. We now know that even the bibliography was phony. It eventually came out that *Why England Slept* was paid for by Kennedy's father in collusion with the influential columnist Arthur Krock; for the Pulitzer Prize–winning *Profiles in Courage*, a historical analysis of great American policy moments gaining him much intellectual cachet, all the basic research and writing were done by advisor and speechwriter Theodore Sorenson. Politically, at home and abroad Kennedy was a policy hip shooter of the worst sort, on the two most important issues of his presidency, making up his civil rights positions by public-relations stagecraft, and getting us into Vietnam by jabbing a macho cold-warrior finger at the map. Psychologically, he was a cynical manipulator of persons, images, and events. Sexually, he was an insatiable seeker of conquests for whom the words *philanderer* and *womanizer* really don't do justice. There aren't enough names to describe all the Jack Kennedys operating under the cool, elegant, stylish persona: a politico, a satyr, a pig, the lace-curtain Irish bootlegger's second son taking steroids for Addison's disease and then fucking himself blind—with bimbos in the White House swimming pool, starlets at the Las Vegas Rat Pack orgies, Marilyn Monroe, Cord Meyer's wife, Sam Giancana's mistress—into needing steady antibiotics for chronic nonspecific urethritis. Meanwhile, he went to Vienna so unprepared that Nikita Khrushchev wound up easily cleaning his clock. With his withdrawal of a U.S. naval umbrella, he left Castro at his leisure to shoot down the Bay of Pigs invaders on the beaches and send the ones escaping annihilation off to die in prison. Meanwhile, down at the Montgomery bus station, John Lewis was getting his brains beaten out by the Klan. And over in Saigon, a bare three weeks before Dallas, Vietnamese leaders Ngo Dinh Diem and Ngo Dinh Nhu got bullets in the head in the back of an armored personnel carrier.

So what's left to care about for some old idealist living on the dark side of Camelot? Well, I do still care about the recklessness. I do still care about the cynicism. But mostly I don't care about him so much as I still care about us, the ones who went for it and in the process truly went for him to places like Philadelphia, Mississippi, or Lai Khe, Vietnam, or Lagos, Nigeria. Who joined the Congress of Racial Equality or the Student Nonviolent Coordinating Committee; the U.S. Army or the U.S. Marines; the Peace Corps, the State Department, the U.S. Agency for International Development, the Committee of Responsibility to Save War-Burned and War-Injured Vietnamese Children. Who committed themselves to public service careers in politics, law, medicine, education, justice, social work, the armed forces, and public administration. I care about all of us and all of our children who now have no choice but to go into a kind of perpetual acceptance mode about government as a source of vulgar amusement—all the nutcake Nixon stuff, Nancy Reagan's astrologers, Bill Clinton's Oval Office blow jobs. But most of all, Kennedy in particular makes me care about something I can't ever stop caring about—and that is the sheer amount of our own youth we were willing to squander on him and his example, on our incredible, heartfelt willingness to become citizens in a country led by a president who turned out to be someone like him.

We may now call the thing a swindle and curse our idiocy, but even now it is hard not to remember the power of the infatuation. Philip Caputo puts it well: "For Americans who did not come of age in the early sixties, it may be hard to grasp what those years were like—the pride and overpowering self-assurance that prevailed." The combination of what he rightly calls "missionary idealism" and power was just irresistible. "America seemed omnipotent then."

For most of that generation of Kennedy idealists, it has all been downhill from there: Vietnam; urban riots; secret government surveillance; Watergate, Iran-Contra; for traditional Republicans, the rise of the fundamentalist, neoconservative Right; for Democrats, a parade of disasters—Johnson, Humphrey, McGovern, Carter, Mondale, Dukakis, Clinton. It remains no small irony for those of us who came of age as Kennedy idealists—first Jack and then Bobby—that the last vestige of the era is a parody of a parody. The last brother, Teddy, is so thoroughly a relic of time that the mention of his own unheroic version of the Kennedy past, including the dead woman and the long-ago swim at Chappaquiddick, brings a glaze to the eyes of anyone under forty. On the evening news there he remains, the great, hulking roseate gasbag, spewing old party platitudes, summoning up one more gasp of liberal indignation. Gore Vidal had it right: he would have made a great bartender.

So here we are, many of us from the Kennedy era, stuck in our own memories of a world that often now looks like a bad movie of itself, one in which we are both the stars and the objects of parody. It is perpetual homecoming at Faber College, in *Animal House*, and we are at the parade at the end of the movie. The interfraternity council president, all prepped out in his Ivy League suit, button-down shirt, and repp tie, shares the reviewing stand with the mayor and the dean, the model marriage of student politics and government, Kennedy youth meets Hitler youth. A parade float blazoning the theme of "The New Frontier" carries sorority-girl Jackies in pink Chanel suits—parodying the blood-soaked one that the stunned, silent widow wore home from Dallas—with matching pillbox hats. We of course prefer the incorrigible Deltas, with their death-star cruiser and dirty parade tricks; but they're really not Ken Kesey–style merry pranksters, either, so much as closet idealists. One will become an OB-GYN, another a U.S. senator. All the young people at Faber College are Kennedy youth; but most of the Kennedy youth at Faber College are really young Republicans. Nothing could be more depressing than this ending of one of the funniest movies ever made.

Nor, in hindsight, are things any less dispiriting when one moves to that foreshadowed future; the youth generation so depleted has produced its own sad parade of would-be JFK imitators. Here, too, for many of us, fighting the political wars of the 1960s and 1970s all over again, we now find only the quadrennial heartsickness of trying to fend off the latest rich, smug, mean Republican bastard with a slick little careerist like Clinton or a leftover *PT-109½* wannabe like Kerry. Clinton. The utter debacle of failed promise goes into déjà vu mode in the snapshot of the famous teenage Clinton handshake with Kennedy from Boys Nation. The Arkansas kid stares at the president in rapture, the stars in his eyes recalling some Sudeten Czech or Anschluss Austrian looking up at the Hitler motorcade. The Rhodes scholar goes to Yale Law and becomes the boy governor. The boy governor becomes the Comeback Kid, the best pure politician of a generation, a bona fide happy warrior in both the FDR and JFK traditions, with the gorgeous rhetoric, the lovely manners, the spellbinding charm. And the sexual rapacity and the political cynicism. The administration falls apart and so do the policy dreams. The second-rate sex scandals meld into Whitewater, playing out into sexual-harassment lawsuits and blow jobs in the Oval Office and the threat of a perjury indictment for making a false statement in a deposition.

Or Kerry (Gore doesn't count, being really a Republican in disguise). Playing to the right, this one does the whole navy hero thing right down to the Vietnam Swift Boat and the reunited "band of brothers" campaign tour. On the left, he reprises the Vietnam Veterans Against the War credentials, the congressional testimony, the long hair, the fatigue jacket. In the middle somewhere is the prep school–Ivy League stuff, this time St. Paul's and Yale. One takes in the jutting jaw, the jabbing finger, the fine manners, practiced cerebrality, the upwardly inflected New England accent and demeanor, somehow mixed in with all the upper-class athleticism, bicycling, snowboarding, wind-surfing. John Forbes Kerry. JFK. Yes, he is a Forbes. Never mind that on the other side the name is not really Irish but a transliteration of Kohn from Austro-Hungarian forebears, Jewish converts to Catholicism, including a grandfather who committed suicide at the Copley in Boston. The whole business is decidedly conflicted, and charmless. The candidate is ponderous, a stiff. One's most ludicrous, even absurd memories of the campaign remain those of John Kerry trying to be JFK-like around grizzled old Vietnam vets, steelworkers, mine workers, trying to act and talk like a regular guy.

"Hey, man," he intones. The JFK is in his dreams; the image is *Saturday Night Live* memories of Steve Martin and Dan Aykroyd as Czechoslovak Swingers.

So what remains? Certain phrasings are still foisted upon us, now utterly without irony. "The Best and the Brightest" lately described the senior honor society at the local high school. "Torino Passes the Torch," read one headline at the close of the 2006 Winter Olympic Games. Beyond that, one might lay claim to a certain quality of elegiac memory. A well-known exchange from the hours of grief following the assassination, for instance, is that reported by Daniel Patrick Moynihan: "We'll never laugh again," a friend wailed. Moynihan is said to have replied, "Oh, we'll laugh again; we'll just never be young again." Well, in retrospect, that is partly true and not bad, either, as anecdotes go. But there was also decidedly something much bigger than that, for the generation that lived through it all. Call it illusion if one will; but it was also, genuinely — in the fullest and deepest way we use that term in American English — something we call myth. For us, the Kennedy myth turned out to be abidingly true in its way, the *PT-109* stuff tied in with the Henry V band of brothers stuff; the 22 November 1963 Dallas assassination stuff tied in with the Romeo and Juliet good night sweet prince stuff; the Robert Frost at the inauguration stuff; the A. E. Housman athlete dying young stuff, by way of the Pablo Casals in the White House stuff, by way of the Caroline and John-John in the Oval Office stuff, with just a little Honey Fitz thrown in on the side. In America, one could say, there had truly been nothing like it in the world before or after. Except in novels, where F. Scott Fitzgerald's Jay Gatsby comes to mind; or in comic books, Superman; or in novels and movies, maybe James Bond. It may well be now just one more illusion we have to get over. Whatever it was, it once thrilled young people all over America with its message and set a lot of us driving through the night from our hometowns and colleges to be there at the end. It's just that now it all seems so, well, sophomoric.

The Best and the Brightest, Only Dumber

When the time comes to write some large, historically contextualized study of the people in positions of authority in America who gave us the Iraq War, I nominate my present title, imaging David Halberstam's magisterial text on the making of the Vietnam debacle (*The Best and the Brightest*), as at least a frame of thematic suggestion—although in the short run Thomas E. Ricks's *Fiasco* is definitely looking like a contender. Failing the book-weight expertise of the professional historian or international affairs specialist, I have decided to go ahead and at least essay the task.

From the beginning of the Iraq war onward, for many of us who lived through the Vietnam era the most disturbing flashback to have come out of the ever-lengthening military nightmare has lain not just in recurrent fears that they are doing *it* all over again. It lies even more dreadfully in who *they* have turned out to be. *They* have turned out to be the latest version of the people who gave us the phrases Counterinsurgency Warfare, Special Operations, Nation Building, Pacification, and Hearts and Minds (on the news a while back, I actually heard a prominent senator say "light at the end of the tunnel"). In Vietnam, those of us out on what John Ellis called "the sharp end" of combat had a name for people like this. We called them REMFs: rear-echelon motherfuckers. REMFs began in Long Binh or Cam Ranh Bay and stretched back through CINCPAC in Honolulu to Washington DC. Now just fill in Baghdad and Southern Command in Tampa and take it on back again to the Pentagon and the White House. Even as all the old phrases get dreadfully recycled, there *they* are again, as Rick Atkinson has phrased it, full of their "cocksure bellicosity."

As a veteran both of the jungle war in Asia and of the wars of cultural consciousness that followed, I must say I have tried my best to resist Vietnam "parallels" or "lessons." As hard as one may try to banish such ghosts of history and memory, however, among major Washington war makers *and* news makers over the past five years, they now seem to have been almost too vividly reincarnated. To be sure, given the ostentatious anti-intellectualism of the sitting president and the rigid conservatism of most of his chief functionaries in matters domestic and international, future historians may balk at the idea of any such assemblage of scintillating intelligences as those who managed to engineer the tragedy of Vietnam. Still, to many people who remember that earlier, agonizing, endless war, the Bush lineup, including those intransigently present and those strategically (albeit in some cases rather untidily) departed, has now come to look like the dream team of nightmares past.

One begins at the top: a drawling Texas guy in cowboy boots, with major manhood issues, coming off the foregoing presidency of a glib, cerebral Rhodes Scholar *and* sexual cavalier, who fired off some pre–September 2001 missiles at Osama bin Laden and then fiddled with a White House intern as terrorism spread its tentacles. With a war that has become increasingly interminable, one sees the narrowing eyes and hears the drawling cadences of the gunslinger: "The nation is strong! We are united against the inimy. Amurri-cans honor their commitments." It is Lyndon Johnson, the embattled sheriff, cleaning up after the glamour boy, the martyred policy intellectual with the James Bond manners and the flashy oratory. Throughout his career, Johnson wore proudly in his lapel a World War II Distinguished Flying Cross he had been awarded as a congressman on temporary assignment to the navy—for riding in an airplane over an area of the Pacific where enemy airplanes might have been patrolling. It wasn't exactly the Hollywood stuff of the heroic Kennedy legend associated with *PT-109*. (Nor, as things turn out, was the *PT-109* saga itself.) But at the time it was serviceable. Accordingly, for Johnson, as a new president in the wake of an instantly mythologized predecessor, Vietnam became a matter of putting up or shutting up, with the big issue that of geopolitical military credibility: the backdown factor. So, during the immediate aftermath of the September 2001 terrorist attacks on the World Trade Center and the Pentagon, and the rooting out in Afghanistan of the Taliban–Al Qaida axis, Bush—as opposed to his predecessor, Bill Clinton, a bona fide draft dodger—could still claim modest credentials as a Vietnam-era jet jock, albeit safely ensconced stateside in the Texas Air National Guard. At least he wasn't Dan Quayle, Indiana weekend warrior extraordinaire, valiantly serving out his time as an enlisted journalist writing for the unit newsletter. Then came Iraq; and then the thoroughly misguided *Top Gun*–"Mission Accomplished" aircraft carrier stunt; and then the threat, during the reelection campaign, of the Navy Swift Boat guy with the Silver Star, the Bronze Star, three Purple Hearts, and the touring *PT-109½*: "Band of Brothers" campaign act. On top of that, there was the earlier George H. W. Bush wimp factor, an abruptly concluded Desert Storm, and the unfinished business with Saddam Hussein. The echoes were coming in loud and clear. Once a Texas Ranger, always a Texas Ranger; and this time nobody *really* gets to come home until they've nailed the coonskin to the wall.

Second-in-command Cheney, of course, got to rehearse for Iraq 2 by doing the Rumsfeld incarnation during Iraq 1 as secretary of defense. Before that he, too, earned major Vietnam-era REMF credentials. Eminently draftable during the peak years of the conflict, he was the recipient of five, separate, officially requested deferments. One presumes, unlike Pat Buchanan or Newt Gingrich, he felt he just couldn't trust the ever-popular trick knee. He simply had, he explained, "other priorities." Those included becoming CEO of Halliburton, the major civilian contractor currently making boatloads of money for logistical service and construction work in the war zone. And of course he *has* shot at least one person.

In eerie reechoing of Dean Rusk, during the run-up and early stages supporting the current war loyally from afar but mainly excluded from discussions concerning its conduct, was the immensely politic secretary of state, Colin Powell. In the closer military parallel, voicing his objections in the councils of power, but thwarted through interlacing chains of command at the DoD and the White House—until his resignation, at least—like Kennedy's and Johnson's star political general, Maxwell Taylor, he soldiered on. Like Taylor, whose impeccable military credentials were similarly combined with an impressive intellectual grasp of geopolitical policy, Powell was the ideal thinking person's military man cast in the policy role: cerebral, articulate, forbearing, loyal, and dignified; like Taylor, he even wrote books. Now, for all the intelligence, circumspection, and dignity, he will be remembered as the high-level chump who got sandbagged at the United Nations into reading the argument for war from the administration script. A towering figure nostalgically imagined from a world before Iraq or Vietnam, he will always be the George Marshall who might have been.

By now, how can one *not* see how unerringly Donald Rumsfeld has come to mirror Robert McNamara, with the aggressive, ball-bearing logic of the corporate military mind, full of force estimates, cost-benefit analyses, and statistical projections? And, as with the commander in chief, one may factor in again the REMF dreams—in Rumsfeld's case, those of the former naval aviator and Blue Angel wannabe—of the hot pilot who never got to fly the big mission. In the White House and the Pentagon, a jocose camaraderie has conflated the mentality of the executive war manager with that of the jet jock, of the board room with the ready room. And here is the Rumsfeld bonus: unlike the McNamara mind, this one is thwarted by no liberal-intellectual angst. We may expect from Donald Rumsfeld no books in later years agonizing over and/or repenting of a crucial role he has played in the making of a disastrous war. There will be no penitential *In Retrospect* or *Argument without End* here. Unclouded by doubt, the Rumsfeld corporate mentality has been from the outset all bottom-line.

Correspondingly, Condoleeza Rice, as the president's national security advisor—now promoted for her loyal service to secretary of state—has neatly channeled the ghost of McGeorge Bundy, the learned, prodigiously analytic, boy-wonder dean of Harvard College, king of the hard-ass policy paper. This time the star West Wing academic has been female and an African American, the learned, prodigiously analytic, wonder-woman former provost of Stanford. Again, war matters have become the latest expertise of the polymathic genius, the brilliant, Russian-speaking figure skater and concert pianist. How tough-minded can you get? At least Bundy got to play soldier during 1941–45 as an intelligence staff officer. No wonder that at Pleiku in 1965, just after a Communist attack, General William Westmoreland described him as being in "full field-marshal psychosis." Of course that may have been the problem.

As to top military management, like the army's Earle G. "Bus" Wheeler back in the late 1960s, both recent chairmen of the Joint Chiefs of Staff, Marine General Peter Pace, and before him Air Force General Richard G. Myers, seem to have earned their positions as team players, mainly standing behind the defense secretary with ready concurrence in the latest wisdom on the strategic big picture. Before them were the plain-speaking special ops hero, Hugh Shelton, and on the ground, the "soldiers' soldier" General Tommy Franks. Already way back is General Eric Shinseki, the long-range strategic thinker who warned of the limitations of the attack plan and the follow-up, out of the army with fellow serious military thinkers as diverse as Barry McCaffrey and Wesley Clark.

Underlings: once again, a host of lesser operatives have worked diligently within the bureaucratic machine, greasing the gears toward full-scale military commitment. This time we have a whole raft of late-middle-aged guys, civilian and military, who didn't get to play cowboys and gooks in Vietnam or Texas Rangers and ragheads in Desert Storm—celebrated neocons, as they came to be called in their passing moment of celebrity, right-wing geopolitical hardliners now for the most part hustled off to the policy sidelines. Among the number have been celebrated strategic force enthusiasts ranging from Douglas Feith and John Bolton at Defense, Richard Perle at the Council on Foreign Affairs, William Kristol at the flagship publication, *The Weekly Standard.* But the exemplary case, surely, will always remain that of Deputy Secretary of Defense Paul Wolfowitz. Wolfowitz: known even among the faithful as Wolfowitz of Arabia, the policy intellectual straddling worlds of government and academe, and now having acted out, almost too eerily for words, *his* Vietnam-era analogue, Walt Whitman Rostow. The latter, at the time, was another of those Kennedy "Harvards," as Johnson called them. Wolfowitz did his academic time at the Graduate School of International Relations at Johns Hopkins University. As with his predecessor, so enamored of bombing they nicknamed him Air Marshal Rostow, Wolfowitz has played the intellectual point man, the type and image of what beat poet Lawrence Ferlinghetti once styled "the smiling mortician," cheerleading for the policy message and stonewalling questioners with unflappable appearances on the congressional griddle. Nor has such faithful service gone unrewarded. Now, almost incredibly, having moved on to presidency of the World Bank, this Rostow rides off into a Robert McNamara sunset—proof positive that royally screwing up a country and killing thousands of its people can still be a résumé builder.

As to the people on the policy hot spot in-country, the neo-Vietnam casting could not have been more impeccable. Before installation of an interim government, L. Paul Bremer, down to his signature suits and desert boots, reincarnated the impeccably diplomatic Henry Cabot Lodge, the handsome, vigorous, almost boyish American proconsul. With his disbandment of the Iraqi army, the de-Baathification of civilian leadership, and his total underestimation of long-standing political factionalisms as the basis of a power vacuum waiting to fill itself back up with anarchy and terrorism, he was forced to yield to the practiced invisibility of John Negroponte. Now with Negroponte rewarded by elevation to a new meganational security post at home, a successor is back in the news: Zalmay Khalilzad, an Afghan native, a neoconservative, and a Sunni Muslim. Having achieved American proconsul status as a miracle worker in the land of his birth, he now receives anointment as the new apostle of Iraqification – as if for the first time suggesting an administration discovery that someone holding the ambassadorship might profit from in-country cultural experience, understanding, or expertise.

Apace, in dizzying succession, counterpart figures in the top military command roles have come and gone, serving their time in the media spotlight and then hustled off-camera when no longer useful. The first occupation commander, accorded a carefully managed midrange celebrity, was a kind of Hispanic Creighton Abrams, the unassuming Lieutenant General Ricardo Sanchez, who received much positive media attention for doing the workmanlike business of "boots on the ground" troop command as the war stretched on. Eventually, of course, *he* had to be sacrificed to the prisoner-of-war scandals of Abu Ghraib, replaced by a former deputy army chief of staff, General George Casey, whose name, in keeping with the politics of the war, is increasingly consigned to the middle pages of newspaper and newscast. One-stars and two-stars who led divisions now rotate back in and out as three-star crackerjack troop trainers and civil affairs specialists. Apace, the visibility of the commander in the region, General John Abazaid, once in the spotlight for his intellectual and public-relations skills, not to mention Middle Eastern family origins and fluency in Arabic, has been dimmed to the odd appearance before a congressional committee.

Meanwhile, over at the CIA, again as in the bad old Saigon days, fingers have pointed, heads have rolled, and a whole intelligence apparatus now continues to roil over lousy information gathering and faulty analysis. Again, in the shadows, like a pack of tired old dogs chasing each other's tails, competing agencies and operational subdivisions play out the Vietnam-era confusions of contending jurisdictions, reporting channels, and chains of command. The guilty CIA director, with his "slam-dunk" assurances to the White House about weapons of mass destruction or Al Qaida connections, throws himself on his sword. An administration loyalist is appointed to get the agency back together. Amid major firings, an entire second-line bureaucracy resigns. To assuage memories of J. Edgar Hoover intelligence gathering at home, the FBI is simultaneously recast as part of the apparatus of domestic security. The director, kept over from prewar days, is rendered even more anonymous than he had been. He, the CIA guy, and the new domestic security guy, the latter's position undermined by congressional reports on his agency's poor performance during a succession of hurricane catastrophes, now report to the new head intelligence guy, who turns out to be the Iraq guy preceding the current one. A lightning-rod attorney general is gone. The USA Patriot Act, newly reconfirmed by the Senate and House, remains in effect.

At the same time, in the larger perspective of policy timetables and events, some Vietnam lessons do seem to have sunk in. Whatever the fate of "democracy building," already carefully exorcised has been the specter of guilt over the 1956 nonelections in Vietnam eventuating in an interminable American sponsorship and military presence. Elections have taken place. A new government is forming. Political victory has been declared in advance. Whether it has already been worth three thousand Americans killed or as many as 150,000 Iraqi lives remains a question also carefully avoided. Ambushes, booby traps, sniper attacks, suicide bombings, and car explosions continue. American soldiers go out every day to kill and die in the name of pacification. Security forces being trained ARVN-like in the American shadow are touted as increasingly "effective," "combat-ready," "good to go." "We will stand down," the saying now goes, "as the Iraqis stand up."

To be sure, it seems unlikely that what is happening in Iraq will ever be a war of national liberation in the sense that Vietnam was one — responding both to a nationalism millennia in the making and the spiritual solidarity born of a people's revolution of workers and peasants. Militarily—albeit of little solace to soldiers doing the dying—in contrast to the expert, well-disciplined Vietcong and North Vietnamese army forces, insurgent fighters in Iraq, for all their murderousness, will continue to be for the most part tactically atomized and reckless. They began by running around in open view with AK-47s and RPGs and allowing themselves to get targeted and killed in droves. They have now been reduced to lethal, largely isolated acts of terror, while inviting equally violent military response frequently turning civilian populations against them as well. But again in the broad prospect, according to Niall Ferguson, if for different reasons, this war for Americans and Iraqis continues to have every prospect of proving at least as bad as the long-term debacle eventually turning most of Indochina into a mass killing ground: a nightmare of competing histories, of jumbled-together warring ethnicities, postcolonial grievances, rivalries, and hatreds; and murderous factionalisms, regionalisms, and nationalisms, likely destabilizing the Middle East for the next half century. U.S. Democratic presidential candidate John Kerry deemed it a major campaign promise in 2004 to assert that he would have American combat formations out of the place within four years. Senator John McCain, back near the beginning, projected the necessity of a military presence for the next one or two decades. Eric Shinseki set half a million troops as a rational estimate for an effective occupation force. Even before the fall 2006 elections, although the administration denies it, it was clear to everyone that not only would we leave Iraq, but that as we leave we would declare victory. Read, "Vietnamization"; or in this case, civil war, Sunni versus Shia, in a truly accursed religious and political feud roughly twelve centuries old that we happened to step into about four years ago. Among the great bad movies of history, as Ferguson proposes, if our current war planners in Washington DC are not watching *Apocalypse Now*, they might still want to consider renting *Lawrence of Arabia*.

One must admit that, back in Washington, the policy dreamers do also seem to have learned a few things about fighting-soldier morale. Troops, many of them now on second assignments, have mainly gone and come back as units; although the deployment cutoff seems now to be a year or so, there is no 365-day tour of duty, scared, anonymous individual replacements thrown in with combat buddies looking out for each other and cynical short-timers. (Actually, under a "stop-loss" policy of involuntary extensions in enlistments and tours of duty, it is now the short-timers who are often more nervous in the service than the new arrivals.) There is well-publicized counseling for returnees, with encounter and therapy groups—although, as a series of *New York Times* articles have reported, still coming home wounded in body and soul when faced with the realization that nobody really much cares. In the public-relations element, a nice touch, particularly during the period of active, major-unit combat, lightning advances and capture of major cities, was the concept of embedded reporters. Thus was forestalled, even for the legendary liberal press, the possibility of a quick adversarial relationship; and now more than three years later, as regards the fighting troops, it is one that still hasn't developed to any great extent. Similarly, in a reversal of an earlier military and public relations decision, much has been made, for good and ill, of the mobilization for combat zone duty of the reserves and national guard – as opposed to making them a haven for persons willing to do military service but avoid active combat. This has been a good decision as far as general morale is concerned, a demonstration in some way of a basic fairness in the distribution of military service. It is also, however, one of the reasons, especially after all the images of the handful of reservists and guardsmen involved in the scandal at Abu Ghraib – poor, rural, uneducated, undertrained – that the role of weekend warriors in-country, now more than forty percent of total strength, has remained less than an occasion for public rejoicing. There has been the occasional mutiny. Back home, stories have surfaced of citizen-soldier domestic hardship, job loss, foreclosures, bankruptcies, and the like. As to the conventional forces arrayed in the field, there can be no gainsaying that these soldiers and marines constitute one of the best and most professional armies America has ever committed to combat. Yet it is hard not to notice that it is a great active-duty army with much the same composition of that which we sent to Vietnam: professional senior officers, young West Point and ROTC captains and lieutenants, a dependable cadre (until they are depleted by multiple tours) of senior NCOs; and then the grunts – brave, hardy nineteen-year-old kids from little places in the South, the new rust-belt Midwest, the tough Northeast, who couldn't find jobs or the money to go to college. For all the fine talk of a volunteer army, our policy of who winds up fighting in Iraq has really boiled down to conscription by other means. You certainly won't see Rumsfeld's or Wolfowitz's nephews and nieces there.

If this war is not the Vietnam of the 1960s nightly news, certainly it is neither the video-game war of 1990–91, where images and reports were tightly controlled. At present, any putative connection between militant Islam and international terrorism remains sufficient basis for most Americans to absorb a finite number of combat casualties. The payback element has also been carefully factored in. What are two or three fully armed, allegedly volunteer American soldiers a day, ten a week, still only around three thousand for a whole war, when nearly the same number of defenseless, unsuspecting civilians died in the Twin Towers? We can also count on masked terrorists to reply with car bombs and hostage murders. From a hole somewhere on the Afghanistan-Pakistan border, Osama bin Laden sends out his latest megalomaniac home video. Failing all these wavings of the bloody shirt, we are now endlessly reminded about the despotism of Saddam Hussein and how, at the very least, the world is better off without him. It is the classic post hoc, ergo propter hoc, nonsense that they know we always fall for, the political and rhetorical equivalent of bait and switch. If none of the initially espoused justifications work out, find one that at least sounds good and supply it after the fact.

This last is vintage Washington logic, and it is not just the people in power who are guilty of it. Now that we find ourselves in this mess, we all look for ways—with which we are happily supplied by our leaders and our popular media—for making us not think about the people who are doing the work at the sharp end or the countless Iraqis we are wounding and killing—what one might call the war's collateral damage. It is exactly the same kind of thinking that still puts Americans out there in their gas-guzzling SUVs with their PalmPilots and cell phones. OK, OK, do what you have to, the country bravely responds. Just as long as it's not my kid.

An expression we had in Vietnam signified for us the knowledge one gains of war at "the sharp end" of military action. The word was REMF— you've seen it throughout this book. REMF is how we distinguished field soldiers from support troops. As I've already explained, RE stands for rear-echelon. And I don't have to remind you what MF means. Ask any old soldier: it's always the REMF bastards who want to go in with bayonets unsheathed and guns blazing—just as long, of course, as it's somebody else's kid in the lead battalion.

Now, as then, in Afghanistan and Iraq, the grunts still do what they have always done, which is basically to go out and eat shit and die—as opposed to the current Washington Best and Brightest, sort of—or, at least according to them, in their latest iteration, the Vulcans. The Vulcans. This, according to a 2004 political history by Jim Mann, *The Rise of the Vulcans*, is what Cheney, Rice, Rumsfeld, Wolfowitz, and others are said to have anointed themselves as a military party during the Bush campaign of 2000. And they don't mean the *Star Trek* kind—the dispassionate, analytic, decision-oriented warrior geniuses on a futuristic TV show. They meant the ancient Vulcan, the god of destructive fire. Did anyone check a dictionary of mythology to find out that the Roman Vulcan, like his Greek predecessor, Hephaestus, was considered among the gods ugly, deformed, and moody—corresponding roughly to a Christian devil figure? That he was known chiefly as a cuckold, having had his manhood mocked by Aphrodite, with an anger volcanic in his resentment and distrust of his fellows? Vulcan may have had the firepower, but he got the shaft. Bush's war cabinet should have stuck with TV. Then, in trying to call themselves Vulcans, they would not have shown how completely, no matter which way their war eventually turns out, they were just another bunch of REMFs.

Hopeless in Honolulu

Honolulu, late November 2005: keeping a steady but comfortable pace –
that of an average, reasonably healthy, late-middle-aged person – I find
I can walk from Waikiki Beach to the top of Diamond Head in about an
hour. For someone like me in my sixties, born during the Battle of the
Philippines in 1944, who grew up on books about the great Pacific War
such as *Guadalcanal Diary*, *Thirty Seconds over Tokyo*, or, most germane to
the view at hand, *Day of Infamy*, it seems as if you can see history itself
from up there. Just to the west of downtown is Pearl Harbor. To the east
is Hanauma Bay, and beyond that, Koko Head. You suddenly realize
that major waves of attacking Japanese planes on Sunday, 7 December

1941, had come straight out of the direction of the imperial homeland called by their pilots "Nihon" or "sun origin." At this time of year, you can also see that the early morning sun rising from that direction is in fact utterly blinding. If you had been down at sea level in Pearl Harbor you would have been looking right into a million shooting rays. You couldn't have seen a Japanese plane coming at you, as they say, if your life depended on it.

For me, this trip to the islands was wrapped up in personal history as well. At a conference marking the thirtieth anniversary of the fall of South Vietnam to the North Vietnamese Communists, I was to read a paper on the history of American representations of the Vietnam War in literature, film, and other popular culture media—a subject to which I had devoted much of my academic career.

It was my third visit to Honolulu. My first had been on a military R & R leave from Vietnam in 1969. After six months in the jungle as an armored cavalry platoon leader, I had started my stay at a luxury hotel in Kahala where some of my most vivid memories involved teenagers from New Jersey complaining loudly about getting fruit instead of potato chips with their cheeseburgers at the swimming pool snack bar. Halfway through my stay I had moved around to the other side of the island, far away from the city and the major tourist areas. By my second visit in the mid 1980s, Waikiki had become a labyrinth of concrete canyons. On a trip to some of the outer islands, where I had particularly wanted to see the old Maui whaling port of Lahaina, out of which Herman Melville had sailed in the 1840s, I found to my great sadness that the whole village had been turned into a boutique.

In Honolulu in 2005, according to recent figures, seventy percent of the people vacationing on Waikiki were Japanese. I could believe that. At the Moana, the Royal Hawaiian, or a number of other major wedding destinations, package deals pumped out three or four couples an hour: the whole drill, happy families, bridesmaids, ushers, formal dress, flowers, champagne, hors d'oeuvres, white stretch limousine, the big bouquet toss, the happy getaway to the honeymoon. Coffee bars and convenience markets were awash in hyperstimulated Asian teenagers, music streaming through their earPods, giggling together and checking messages on cell phones. Entire clans on the sidewalk – mothers, fathers, grandparents, children – moved intently with the hustle and flow, surging ahead in cohesive clusters, breaking right or left to avoid colliding with fastwalkers coming the other way.

What I noticed most of all this time, however, were the Americans – so many of them, in depressingly visible contrast, big, slow-moving, overfed, and joyless. On Waikiki itself, no one wore a bathing suit. The standard costume was shorts and oversize T-shirts. Most often they moved by couples, pairs of men and women so heavy in body and spirit that they walked with visible effort. Just breathing seemed to exert them, and their flushed skins carried a toilsome sheen of perspiration. But it was the eyes that told the story. They too carried a glaze – of stunned, unblinking, utterly incurious stultification. Meanwhile, I had the odd impression that this could be happening anywhere in America – at Universal Studios in Orlando, Florida, or at O'Hare International Airport in Chicago, Illinois; at the Bruno's prescription counter in my hometown of Tuscaloosa, Alabama; or in a line of people buying automobile tags in Hagerstown, Maryland, or Pullman, Washington. From any of these places one could now send a postcard of the view. Welcome to fat-ass nation, it might read – describing a condition of body and spirit permeating to the core of American being. Welcome to the empire of terminal ingestion and acquiescence: where we are fat because we eat too much, drive everywhere, get little or no exercise, and put our hope in fad diets and weight-loss surgery, when the simple fact is that we take in far more calories than we are able to burn; where we are stupid because we think too little and believe too much, letting others do our thinking for us in ways that make us relish ignorance and misinformation, slop it up from the latest political or religious nincompoop by the bowl or bucketful.

Or, as Charles Pierce has written in "Greetings from Idiot America":

A federally funded abstinence program suggests that HIV can be transmitted through tears. An Alabama legislator proposes a bill to ban all books by gay authors. The Texas House passes a bill banning suggestive cheerleading. And nobody laughs at any of it, or even points out that, in the latter case, having Texas ban suggestive cheer-

leading is like having Nebraska ban corn. James Dobson, a prominent conservative Christian spokesman, compares the Supreme
Court to the Ku Klux Klan. Pat Robertson, another prominent
conservative preacher, says that federal judges are a more serious
threat to the country than is Al Qaeda and, apparently taking his text
from the Book of Gambino, later sermonizes that the United States
should get with it and snuff the democratically-elected president of
Venezuela.

The Congress of the United States intervenes to extend into a
televised spectacle the prolonged death of a woman in Florida. The
majority leader of the Senate, a physician, pronounces a diagnosis
based on heavily edited videotape. The majority leader of the House
of Representatives argues against cutting-edge research into the use
of human stem cells by saying that "an embryo is a person. . . . We
were all at one time embryos ourselves. So was Abraham. So was
Muhammad. So was Jesus of Nazareth." Nobody laughs at him or
points out that the same could be said of Hitler, Stalin, Pol Pot, or
whoever invented the baby-back rib.

Pierce's essay, oddly, begins as a travel narrative. He is visiting a
natural-history theme park in Tennessee illustrating the principles of sci-
entific creationism. Among its more striking features is that the prehis-
toric humans in the displays walk around with dinosaurs. Pierce's larger
point could not be more clear. The name of the game is willed idiocy.
In a country once renowned for its inventive bravery and enterprise in
looking at human problems and trying to solve them head-on, few in the
populace now remain who have sufficient curiosity to seek even the most
rudimentary knowledge. If anything, in matters as diverse and pressing
as global warming or stem cell research, people actually seem afraid of
information that might be the result of sustained thought or expertise. In
a world where knowledge and basic information are there for the taking
as never before, we enjoy being Idiot America, a place where we are
free to be intentionally stupid, intransigently stupid, even aggressively
stupid.

All I can say is that from his opening vignette onward, Pierce and I seem to be fellow travelers in the land of the big reality show: an America where any attempt at cultural critique has to work hard to move beyond the figure of its own obviousness. For many of us who went through the 1960s, even the great old titles don't do it justice. How does one even begin to write a book like Herbert Marcuse's *One-Dimensional Man* in a nondimensional world? Or Norman O. Brown's *Life against Death* for people who are not even alive enough to know they're dead? At every layering of cultural memory, it just gets worse. No young person knows enough even to relate to a title like *Growing Up Absurd.* No elder has the modicum of self-awareness to recognize a life of quiet desperation.

Nor, in my own case, is any of this helped by my being an old Vietnam grunt with a survivor-head–the concomitant mixture of sadness and fury that one frequently feels about lives lived in poverty, disease, fear, and suffering–but as often not lived at all because of a monumental lack of self-awareness. You watch people go through a natural disaster, a bad illness, an abusive relationship, some other kind of traumatic event, a severe injury, a robbery, an assault, an accident, the loss of a loved one; you watch others stumbling around in the world with that vacancy in their faces, looking at nothing, dying of their own terminal stupefaction. You want to say to everyone, here we all are, at least, breathing in and breathing out.

The fact of the matter is that, as I grow older, I encounter moments in life when I actually think I have slipped into one of the final scenes of William Styron's *Sophie's Choice*: the memorial service arranged by the narrator, Stingo, for his friends, the doomed beautiful lovers of the novel, Sophie and Nathan. Stingo has dug up an interfaith minister about whom he knows nothing; the minister knows nothing about Sophie or Nathan and nothing about love and death, save as the subjects of his own existential platitudes. In his eulogy, the minister honks and drones about "lost children," "victims of an age of rampant materialism," "loss of universal values," "failure of the old-fashioned principles," "*inability to intercommunicate.*" Somewhere in the midst of this, Stingo falls asleep and begins to dream. With a start, he is awakened by another voice. He hears someone saying, "*What fucking bullshit.*" The person he hears is himself.

Such was the personal mix of memory and reflection I had carried to the old island paradise in 2005. And so, in response to the terms of my professional invitation, I found myself disposed to a correspondingly dismal tenor of public pronouncement—especially when it seemed that so much of the bad history I knew so intimately was now marching back to meet me from halfway around the globe. I had come to assert the importance of addressing the cultural legacies, as recorded in history, literature, and film, of a misbegotten geopolitical adventure resulting in the deaths of 58,000 Americans and between two and four million Vietnamese; and now, thirty years after the fall of Saigon, misled by a new cabal of Washington militarists into a catastrophic war on the basis of nonexistent evidence about weapons of mass destruction and unsubstantiated rumors about Al Qaida connections, we found ourselves struggling to extricate ourselves from the latest bloody mess in Baghdad. By 2005 the War on Terror had become real in a way even the Cold War had never been. Two missing skyscrapers in New York, a hole in the Pentagon, and a burning airplane in a field in Pennsylvania—not to mention three thousand dead Americans—testified to that. Nor could anyone deny the justifications for the military takedown of the Taliban in Afghanistan and the now perpetual hunt for bin Laden. Yet seizing on such pretexts, a militaristic administration had decided to make Mesopotamia safe for democracy. What it got instead was the latest blowup of the old nightmare myths of American historical innocence and geopolitical invincibility. Nearly four years into a meat-grinder war combining the worst features of political and religious insurgencies, nearly three thousand Americans were dead and twenty thousand plus wounded. A military walkover had tailed into an endless insurrection of suicide bombers, improvised explosive devices, ambushes, snipers, and booby traps, picking off five or ten Americans a week. Among Iraqis, civilian casualties of sectarian violence continued to pile up literally beyond counting. Casualties of thirty or forty, fifty or sixty people a day blown apart, burned, shot, tortured, mutilated, barely merited a headline. My conclusion about any insight to be distilled from my particular installment in the history of American wars and American peace—after three decades of reading and writing and hoping for something worthwhile to come of it—was that we were doing it all over again; and, that further, unless it was someone's kid or cousin in uniform, father or mother, uncle or aunt, the average American couldn't care less.

Thus I prepared to speak in Hawaii both as a veteran of an old war and as a lifelong chronicler and exegete of its cultural representations, with the shadow of one piece of bad history brooding over another. "Thirty Years After: The Archaeologies"—this was the official title of my 2005 lecture. Scheduled as the final presentation of the three-day symposium, it had shaped itself over months of research and writing as a late-career retrospective: a kind of valedictory overview of primary works on the Vietnam War in history, literature, and film, and of a vast body of critical and theoretical study on cultural representations. As the concluding event on the program, it was also to respond to the presentations of three featured artists: the novelist Tim O'Brien, long regarded as the literary laureate of my generation of the war; the poet and translator Wayne Karlin, a pioneering publisher of works by American and Vietnamese writers; and the young Vietnamese exile writer Andrew Lam, representing a new generation of response to the cultural legacies of the conflict. Further, it was to attempt a plenary response to a body of small-group scholarly presentations at the conference, their relevance to American cultural values and attitudes, current issues of war and peace.

As I completed my work of summation and critique in that final plenary, I found myself surprisingly invigorated, energized, even inspired. Thirty years after the Vietnam War, the archaeologies of knowledge seemed to be shaping and enlarging themselves as a work in significant progress. The featured writers had given readings from their works to large, enthusiastic audiences, and had made stimulating oral presentations. Young American academic scholars and critics proved themselves not simply to be schooled in Vietnamese life and culture, history and politics, but also in many cases to have their learning undergirded by formal literacy in Vietnamese language. Many American and Asian speakers revealed deep connections in Vietnamese American communities, both exile and postexile; some were frequent travelers to Vietnam, self-instructed in the strange navigations required in the world of the People's Republic. All of the younger people seemed to know the standard texts of history, literature, and film backward and forward; they were further distinguished by their masteries of new theoretical discourses, research skills, and media technologies, working fluidly in forms of critical and . cultural inquiry—as I reminded them—that had been barely invented thirty-five years ago when I returned to graduate school after Vietnam. Their presentations frequently struck me, I suggested, not so much as second-generation work as perhaps third or fourth.

But I had to confess at the end of my talk that my own thoughts over the years had been moving me steadily in a different direction. And that it had turned out to be a direction beyond valedictory. In essence I confessed to the whole company that I now no longer believed in anything I had once said about the moral or political efficacy of the writings of the Vietnam War in particular or about literary expression in general. I said that the real title of my lecture should have been "Hopeless in Honolulu."

I recalled aloud that at a 1985 Asia Society Symposium in New York marking ten years after the end of the Vietnam War I had spoken the following words: "We can truly be transformed, and even possibly redeemed, by electing to write at times of what happened—but also of what might have happened, what could have happened, what should have happened, and also what can be kept from happening or what can be made to happen. . . . Words are all we have." Back in 1985 I had further noted their origin in words to similar effect spoken at the conference by another attendee, the novelist Tim O'Brien, who in turn had made an earlier version of them, in *Going After Cacciato*—a work for which he had won the National Book Award—the words of his fictional protagonist Paul Berlin. "What, in fact," Berlin asks himself, "had become of Cacciato? More precisely—as Doc Peret would insist that it be phrased— more precisely, what part was fact and what part was the extension of fact? And how were facts separated from possibilities? What had really happened and what merely might have happened? How did it end?"

I told my 2005 audience that I had elaborated that concept into the thesis of a book on my generation of writers of the war, centering it on what I proposed to be their collective new faith in the transforming and redeeming power of fictions, and on the consequent emergence of a literature uniquely combining the experiential and the imaginative into new forms of literary truth telling, navigating between the leaden horror of the quotidian and the airy excesses of postmodern preciosity.

Now, in Hawaii I confessed that I no longer believed any such thing, and that I despaired basically of literature's making sense of anything. I confessed that I now saw on one hand a world where fictions—what we might call ways of finding things out about the world—had become relentlessly codified into violently contending myths—total and adequate explanations of things as they are and were; and that I looked out on the other into a morass of pain and suffering where on any given day one could only feel overwhelmed by the brute intransigence of fact; that, in the new age of American empire, as a human person in history, on most days I just felt a long way from anywhere, like the infantryman in the soldier story, shot dead but too dumb to fall down; that, as to current matters of American wars and American peace, the nation seemed to be pretty much back at the same bottom line of three decades earlier—the old one about American mission and the dream of dominion over history. After all these years, we just didn't really seem to have learned much of anything.

At the end, I told my audience that I was handing the work over to them. Meanwhile, I tried rhetorically to make something of a constructive exit. I went for the dotage thing. I pretended to resurrect some of the old grunt bravado—declaiming on the virtues of what Paul Fussell calls the pissed-off infantryman's eternal duty to say no to bullshit. Alternatively, I touted the merits of a certain late-life acceptance. I quoted Siegfried Sassoon, thirty-odd years after his war—then called the Great War—finding himself actually attracted, as he put it, to "the idea of oblivion." "I want, after life's fitful fever," he said simply, "to sleep."

At length, I confessed to a peculiar nostalgia. On many days, I said, my mind had started going back to a much earlier time and place and world, complete with high hopes and a clear-channel top-forty soundtrack. I cited one more text:

"There was a song called 'Runaway' by a guy named Dell Shannon playing one Saturday at the baseball field. I remember it was a beautiful spring day and we were young back then and really alive and the air smelled fresh. This song was playing and I really got into it and was hitting baseballs and feeling like I could live forever."

The passage I identified as the concluding paragraph of Ron Kovic's *Born on the Fourth of July.* The memory, I said to the conference attendees, must surely be that of every veteran: that of a world where the war hadn't happened yet.

Those were my concluding words, and at the time I meant them sincerely as part of a larger renunciation. Yet even as I pronounced them, it should have been clear to me that once again I had gotten there only with the help of somebody else's words; and it should have been equally clear to me that, for all my protestations, I had come to that place in some modest hope that my words, for good or ill, might still find an echo. To put this simply, I had wound up sabotaging my own ulterior design. My words had betrayed me. "Hopeless in Honolulu" notwithstanding, there I was, in my own version of a Rick Bragg anecdote from the projects in New Orleans, holding on to the small faith of those crazy for meanings: still trying to write it down so people remember.

A Note on Sources

Information in "Pax Americana" on current U.S. military deployments world-wide is available on the official U.S. Department of Defense Web site (http://www.defenselink.mil/). In "Top Gun and the Tank Driver," my account of the presidential fly-in and "Mission Accomplished" speech is compiled from *New York Times* news stories and follow-up reports. Personal and family information concerning the death of Private First Class Jesse Givens and the posthumous citation of his letters is taken from the "Fallen Heroes of Operation Iraqi Freedom" Web site (http://www.fallenheroesmemorial.com/), including links to media reports and a message section posting exchanges between Givens's family and numerous respondents.

In "An Old GI Looks at Generation Kill," the latter phrase is taken from the main title of Evan Wright's journalistic account of his experiences while embedded with a marine scout platoon spearheading the 2003 U.S. invasion of Iraq (*Generation Kill: Devil Dogs, Iceman, Captain America, and the New Face of American War*, New York: G. P. Putnam's Sons, 2004). "The Sharp End" is the title of John Ellis's classic account of close combat in World War II (*The Sharp End of War: The Fighting Man in World War II*, North Pomfret, Vermont: David & Charles, 1980). The *New York Times Magazine* report by Jim Lewis on a Qatar R&R center for Iraq war troops appeared on 28 August 2005. General Barry McCaffrey's comments on the demands of multiple combat tours by volunteer soldiers have been a recurrent theme of his reflections on the war as a military analyst for NBC television. The *New York Times* article on the failure of the U.S. Army to meet May 2005 recruiting goals appeared on 8 June. Bernard Fall's citation of Menachem Begin among his epigraphs to *Hell in a Very Small Place: The Siege of Dien Bien Phu* (Philadelphia: Lippincott, 1966) condenses a longer phrasing from Begin's *The Revolt: Story of the Irgun*, first published in 1951 (New York: H. Schuman). "When a nation's soul awakens," wrote Begin, "its finest sons are willing to give their lives to ensure success. When an empire is threatened with collapse, it is willing to sacrifice its non-commissioned officers."

In "Squad Leaders in the Sky," the "romping stomping combat stud" line is a typical David Hackworth phrasing in works such as his 1989 memoir, *About Face* (New York: Simon & Schuster). The extended quote from a former infantry battalion commander in Vietnam and subsequent shorter remarks by battalion and company-level officers come from the oral history collection housed at the U.S. Army Military History Institute in Carlisle, Pennsylvania. The typescript staff study cited is by Lieutenant Colonel Kevin Corcoran. It is titled "Maneuver Company Commanders and Their Battalion Commanders in Vietnam: No Shared Value."

In "Home of the Infantry," sources of information on Lieutenant William Calley and the My Lai massacre include the 1971 *Lieutenant Calley: His Own Story [as Told to] John Sack* (New York: Viking); Wayne Greenhaw, *The Making of a Hero: The Story of Lieut. William Calley Jr.* (Louisville: Touchstone, 1971); and *Four Hours in My Lai*, edited by Michael Butler and Kevin Sim (New York: Viking), the follow-up 1998 volume to a remarkable BBC documentary. Local newspaper information on Calley can be found in the historical index of the

Columbus Ledger Inquirer. My understanding of Calley during the court-martial period was enhanced by conversations with Wayne Greenhaw, who is still taking heat from readers who totally missed the irony in his 1971 title. Information on more recent developments in Calley's life came from a phone interview with Richard Hyatt, a staff writer for the *Ledger Inquirer.*

In "Hajis," the "looney tunes" reference for mid-1980s Lebanese terrorist factions comes from Philip Caputo's journalism-based novel, *DelCorso's Gallery* (New York: Holt, Rinehart & Winston, 1983). The *New York Times Magazine* profile of Syrian dictator Bashar al-Assad appeared on 19 July 2005.

In "Swindled by Saint Jack," the "coruscatingly stupid" witticism comes from Benjamin Bradlee's tribute volume, *That Special Grace* (Philadelphia: Lippincott, 1964). The Dean Rusk "other guy just blinked" quote has become a commonplace of lore from the Cuban Missile Crisis. According to the *Presidential Recordings of John Fitzgerald Kennedy*, it may have originated in an aside from Rusk to McGeorge Bundy during a meeting of 24 October 1962. John Hellman's "erotics of a presidency" phrasing comes from *The Kennedy Obsession: The American Myth of JFK* (New York: Columbia University Press, 1997). Philip Caputo's remarks on the romance of the Kennedy presidency appear in his *A Rumor of War* (New York: Holt, Rinehart & Winston, 1977). The Gore Vidal quote about Ted Kennedy appears in *The Portable Curmudgeon Redux* (New York: Dutton, 1992), compiled and edited by Jon Winokur. Vidal is also alleged to have said of Kennedy that every country needs a King Farouk.

Rick Atkinson's "cocksure bellicosity" quote in "The Best and the Brightest, Only Dumber" appears in a 4 April 2004 *New York Times* review, by Christopher Dickey, of Atkinson's book about the Iraq Invasion, *In the Company of Soldiers: A Chronicle of Combat* (New York: H. Holt, 2004). *New York Times* accounts of post-traumatic stress disorder in veterans of the Iraq War began appearing in July and August 2004. Reports have continued to appear regularly, including a December 2006 news story on combat exhaustion in marines serving multiple combat deployments.

The Charles Pierce *Esquire* article cited in "Hopeless in Honolulu" appeared in the November 2005 issue. Paul Fussell's use of the phrase "pissed-off infantryman" has served as a recurrent characterization of his attempts as a writer to debunk mythologies of military manhood. His own pissed-off memoir of World War II infantry combat is titled *Doing Battle: The Making of a Skeptic* (Boston: Little, Brown, 1996). The phrasing of my addition about an "inalienable right to say no to bullshit" is borrowed from Charles Durden's novel of Vietnam War combat, *No Bugles, No Drums* (New York: Viking, 1976). Siegfried Sassoon's late-life reflections appear at the end of *Siegfried's Journey* (New York: Viking, 1946).